A
HEART
NEAR DEATH

A HEART NEAR DEATH

A MEMOIR IN FIVE ACTS

NORMA M. RICCUCCI

authorHOUSE®

AuthorHouse™ LLC
1663 Liberty Drive
Bloomington, IN 47403
www.authorhouse.com
Phone: 1-800-839-8640

Published by AuthorHouse   09/05/2013

ISBN: 978-1-4918-0991-4 (sc)
ISBN: 978-1-4918-0990-7 (e)

Library of Congress Control Number: 2013915010

To my beloved
parents and grandmothers

OVERTURE
CHE GELIDA MANINA
("Your Tiny Hand is Frozen,"
from Puccini's *La Bohème*)

We stood in front of big, black-lacquered double doors. I whimpered and shook uncontrollably, clutching onto my father's arm so tightly that I could almost hear the stitching in his suit jacket popping stitch by stitch. Both doors opened slowly and simultaneously. Mr. LaPorta stood before us with his perfect posture, glossy black shoes, stiffly starched white dress shirt and jet-black suit, a tiny white carnation in its buttonhole.

"Please come in." A smile twitched across his face as he motioned with his outstretched arm, directing us to move to the back of the room. The soft sounds of an organ dirge were being piped into the room from somewhere above my head. I was afraid to open my eyes and buried my face deeply into the crook of my father's arm. I cracked open one eye. Rows upon rows of bright, crimson upholstered folding chairs made of a dark rich wood lined the room.

At the back of the room had been piled a mountain of white flowers in colored pots.

I felt a sudden sense of terror; my body was limp and clammy and I tasted bile creeping up my throat. *What will she look like? Will she be brown and rubbery?* I wanted to run away. But the room was full of people and they were all staring at us.

As we walked toward the back of the room, my mother slowly came into view. She was lying in an enormous, pink satin-lined wooden toy-box chest. The lid above her looked as if it would snap shut at any moment. She was wearing her favorite gold and cream lamé dress with the matching hat. Only the top half of the casket was open, so I could not see her from the hips down. About four feet in front of the casket was a thick, richly varnished wooden kneeling post with red velour-cushioned, knee upholstery that would accommodate at least two grownups or three kids. As we got closer, I shut my eyes again, afraid of her, or maybe just afraid of what death might look like. I slowly opened my eyes and began sobbing. My mother, Tosca, lay motionless on this pillowy mass of pink satin. She was neither smiling nor frowning. But her face looked very peaceful, no longer grimacing from pain or grief.

I wanted to scream out as loudly as I could. Why had God taken her away from me?

In November of 1956, the month and year of my birth, my mother had heard Bellini's *Norma* on the radio in the living room of our Connecticut home. The Metropolitan Opera's Saturday Broadcast presented Maria Callas debuting in the title role and my mother had been utterly taken by the diva's dark, throaty voice singing "Casta Diva." Callas's passion prompted her, not only to name me Norma, but to send my father out for the recording. For years after I was born, she played that LP over and over on our Silverstone Stereo Hi-Fi with the built-in radio.

Bellini's opera tells the story of how a high priestess of the Druids struggles to withstand the suffering and betrayal brought by loved ones in her life. My mother, herself named for another tragic heroine of opera, Puccini's *Tosca*, could have predicted her own young death then or how these same themes would score my life in the years that followed. Although I never walked into a billowing funeral pyre, as Bellini's protagonist does, I, too, as a young woman, was to feel a strange, perverse attraction to death.

Opera would come to be a powerful symbol for me, a touchstone to which I have returned. And while I no longer feel so drawn to death, opera's stories and the powerful music through which they are told have asked me to make life choices—whom to love or not to love; whom to betray or to forsake; whom to forgive. The music grips my soul in its mighty fist. The combination of sounds—melody, harmony, instruments and the exquisite voices, sometimes soft and lilting, other times swelling with thunderous rhapsody—evoke anger, sadness, elation, hopelessness and despair, healing or unfulfilled longing.

When I turn my mind's eye to see my mother in her casket, my hand on my father's arm, and so many more of the hardest moments I have known, I hear these arias.

Opera is the story of my life.

Act I. Scene 1.
Introduzione

("*Introduction*," from Bellini's *Norma*)

I was born with a tiny hole in my heart.

The last of three children and the only girl, I was what my mother had hoped for all along, and the thought of her baby daughter having a physical impairment nearly crushed Tosca Riccucci. Her GP explained that the hole, no bigger than a pinhead, was very common at birth and would not cause me any problems because it was so small. He told her that it would close spontaneously during the first few years of my life. This didn't stop either my mother or my father from pampering and spoiling me. Except for my two brothers, I was my parents' only child.

I was four years old when I got my parents to get us a puppy. All three of us kids wanted a dog, but my brothers put me up to the task of asking for one. My oldest brother Johnny said, "You ask, Norma. They never say no to you." Ricci (pronounced RICH-ee), just 15 months older than I, nodded.

I asked my father first. I knew he'd be easier to convince. "You kids should have a puppy," he agreed.

"Dogs are good for the temperament. They help build character. They're loyal and teach you something about responsibility. But see what your mother says."

Just as we sat down at the dinner table that night, I turned to Mom. "Daddy said we could have a puppy." Furtively, I glanced over at my handsome father, who had stretched out and crossed long fingers from both his hands over his mouth to hide a smile.

My mother didn't even look over at him. She was quiet for a moment, then turned to me and said, "You kids can have a puppy if your father takes me to the Met."

"Oh, pooh," I thought. "Daddy hates opera. Now we'll never get a dog."

Every Saturday afternoon my mother listened to the Metropolitan Opera's Saturday Broadcasts and every Sunday during dinner, she would carefully select and play an opera record from her vast collection. My father invariably made some smart-ass remark about having to listen to a bunch of caterwauling. As my brothers and I laughed, he would mimic the divas, screeching the lyrics in a high-pitched voice, clutching his chest to heighten, for example, the drama of Lucia's mad scene: "*Ohime, sorge il tremendo fantasma e ne separa*": Alas, arises a tremendous phantom and it separates us!

Now, to my surprise, he told my mother, "Okay, Tosca, I'll take you to the Met." A satisfied smile played across her lips and she bowed her head, her long, dark hair hiding her expression. He sighed.

My parents saw Donizetti's *Lucia di Lammermoor* and not a week later, we got our puppy, Bebe, a real mutt. When my father walked through the front door with her, he came to me first and gently placed her in my arms; I squeezed her tightly to my chest. She was beautiful, with short, sandy-brown hair, droopy, buttery-soft ears and big floppy paws. Her warm furry belly rested in my hand, and as she wiggled to escape my clutch, I sniffed her forehead. She smelled like the clean laundry hanging on the clothesline in our backyard. Johnny and Ricci and I loved Bebe instantly.

"Promise to take good care of her now," said my father, my mother standing beside him and smiling despite herself.

My brothers and I swore we would.

Bebe was not our only pet. Two years later, when I was six, my dad came home with a small billy goat. His parents, Giovanni and Maria Riccucci, our Nonno and Nonni Next Door because our brick ranch houses shared a wall, were delighted. My mother and her mother, Nonni Upstairs, who lived in the upper portion of our house, were horrified.

The goat my father brought, with its short scruffy gray beard, looked very old. But he resembled a big, gangling dog and I promptly fell in love with him. I named him Pooch, short for Puccini. Dad also brought with Pooch a rickety little cart. He attached the cart to Pooch, placed Ricci or me inside, and ran alongside Pooch, holding on to the thin bridle draped across his head. Bebe ran with us, too. Along the way, Pooch left tiny little raisin-like shit pellets. Up and down our dead-end street we went. "Like gypsies!" Nonni Upstairs lamented. My father made matters worse by wearing an old, holey sweatshirt, a frayed rope in place of a belt to hold up his baggy, threadbare pants and a moth-eaten Pork Pie hat. Embarrassed, my mother and Nonni Upstairs remained indoors, not even peeking out our picture window to get a glimpse of us running around screaming.

Then, one day, Pooch mysteriously disappeared. Ricci and I were especially upset, and asked our father, "Where's our Pooch?"

He looked at us with his big brown eyes then looked at the sky. "I had to give Pooch away because he was getting too old. Besides, you know he was always escaping from his little pen and eating up all our vegetables from the garden."

But I wondered about the funny tasting meat Nonno and Nonni Next Door served the following Easter Sunday. Johnny blurted out, "Are we eating Pooch?" I looked over at Nonni Next Door, who lowered her head. Nonno just laughed. I let out a loud gasp and ran to our side of the house. Mom followed, trying to console me, but I sobbed into my pillow for the rest of the day. Nonni Upstairs only muttered to her daughter, "You can't expect anything good from the likes of "*gli Riccucci.*"

My paternal grandparents, Nonni Upstairs said, came from a long line of *contadini*: "Just plain old farmers."

She was quick to remind us that *she* was a Manciati—a descendant of the long line of dukes and duchesses of the aristocratic, insular, Manciati family. And that her husband Giovanni, who I never knew, descended from the Caietani family, one of whom—Aloisio Caietani—was a philosopher and contemporary of Dante Alighieri. Caietani, she told us all more often than we cared to hear, was entombed in Florence in the Basilica di Santa Croce, right next to Machiavelli and only a few tombs down from Dante.

Another of my maternal grandfather's ancestors, Nonni said, was a student and disciple of St. Francis of Assisi, and had been memorialized in a small concrete stone in the famous chapel, *Porziuncola*, or "the little portion." The *Porziuncola* is where St. Francis first began his missionary work, preaching the message of poverty, joy and humility. Centuries later, the basilica, Santa Maria degli Angeli, was constructed over the *Porziuncola* as a monument to the life's work of St. Francis and the stone bearing the Catani name remains intact there. The Manciati's and Catani's, Nonni Upstairs would recount in her many stories to us, lived celebrated, consequential lives.

Margherita Elisa Catani, our Nonni Upstairs, unlike most immigrants from Europe in the early 20th century, never wanted to come to America. But in 1921, three years after they married, my grandfather urged her to immigrate. "It's only for a few years, Liza," he assured her. My grandfather was a stonemason. There were jobs for farmers and railway workers but, at the turn of the century in the towns and villages of Florence and other large Tuscan cities, there was no work for stonemasons. The agreement he struck with my grandmother was to live in Hartford, Connecticut, where many Italians had already settled and where accelerated growth and industrialization held the promise of an abundance of jobs for stonemasons. My grandfather would build some buildings, make some money, and then they would return to Italy. He sailed to America, found a job, and six months later sent for my grandmother.

The trip over proved to be her first bad experience with her adopted country. Not only was she prone to motion sickness but she was eight months pregnant with my mother. Her entire trip across the Atlantic Ocean consisted of sleeping and puking, which was, she later maintained, the root cause of her daughter's death. Nonni Upstairs would blame herself when my mom got sick and died. For my grandmother, this rough passage over was a mere overture to the way her life in the United States would be.

Upon arrival at Ellis Island, my grandmother was herded through a maze of what looked to her like cattle stalls—winding, narrow queues, divided by steel railings reaching halfway to the ceiling, with hordes of foreigners whispering in their native tongues, bulging against both sides of the barriers. She waited her turn for the routine questions asked of everyone seeking entry to the U.S. She had memorized in English the answers to the few questions her husband had prepared her for.

> What's your name? *Margherita Elisa Catani.*
> Where are you from? *EE-tully.*
> Are you married or single? *Eye MAAH-reed.*
> What is your occupation? *Eye MAY-cuh da close.*

How much money do you have? Nonni was prepared to flash him a crisp U.S. fifty dollar bill that Nonno had sent her months earlier. The twenty-five dollar rule had been repealed, but it still helped to show some cash.

Nonni didn't have a chance to recite her answers that day. Before she could be interrogated, the immigration doctor grabbed her by the face, pointed it upwards, took a small penlight and peered into her left eye. He flipped the eyelid with a buttonhook, and she shrieked in fear. Then he bellowed, "Eye infection," and marked her shoulder with a big "E" in white chalk. An Italian translator mumbled for her to step to the right and sit in a main hall with all of the other women, who, seated neatly in row upon row of wooden benches, looked just as bewildered as my grandmother. Many had tiny pieces of paper pinned to their clothing with their surnames scrawled in ink pen or in pencil: Batalli, Roskowitz, O'Mallorey, Baumgaertner, Panetta, Rosenbloom, Schneider, Libenitz, MacKenzie, Pagano. Some had a chalked "X" on their shoulder, for possible mental disorder while others were marked with an "L" for lameness, signifying that they hadn't passed the medical exam. Unlike my grandmother, who had two huge *bauli*, or wooden trunks, off to the side where she could keep an eye on them, most had only cloth sacks or small suitcases made of cardboard that sat on the floor nestled in the concaves of their dresses or long skirts, in between their legs. Some of the women cradled crying babies wrapped in thick wool blankets. None of the women cried. They sat stoically, waiting to be told what their next move must be.

Nonni was quarantined with other possibly infectious immigrants and forced to sleep in suffocating, wretched conditions. Dozens of suspect immigrants were cramped into tiny, windowless rooms, without access to bathrooms or washrooms. They slept on tiny, thin canvas hammocks stacked one on top of another that were suspended from the ceiling on rickety, rusty, chrome-linked chains. Other than the muted shuffles of frightened women preparing to spend their first night in this, their putative new country, the rooms were overwhelmed by stillness. My grandmother, awake and queasy from her canvas mat swaying back and forth as a result of the movements of other restless women above her, anxiously thought, "*Oh, my poor, unborn baby; what have I done to you?*" Italians always find a way to blame some*thing* or some*one* when something goes wrong. Often it is "*mia culpa*," blaming oneself for the misfortune. I would eventually blame

Nonni Upstairs for instilling the Italian guilt thing in me. Nonni would not have been heartbroken if she did, in fact, pose a health hazard and was refused entry into America.

A young Italian errand boy was able to get word to my grandfather, who had been waiting patiently a short ferry ride away at the tip of Battery Park for his pregnant wife to gain clearance. It turned out she didn't have an eye infection and was cleared for entry the next day. She was convinced the doctor marked her with an "E" because she emitted a sharp scream when he grabbed her face to examine her eyes; Nonni Upstairs had a story for everything. A month later, she gave birth to my mother, and named her Tosca for her favorite opera. I often heard Nonni say, in her customary, sardonic way, and not at all concerned that she was being crass, "A-MAAH-ree-cah, A-MAAH-ree-cah . . . *una merda*." She had not yet learned enough English to say "SHIT-eh."

Nonni Upstairs was stubborn. One of her many subtle forms of protest against living in America was that she outright refused to learn the English language. "I learned enough to get into America," she would say; "that's all I need to know." While most of her *paesani* were attending night classes to learn English, Nonni Upstairs bided her time until she could return with her family to Italy. Because she lived in an Italian enclave in Hartford—Goodman Place—where all of her neighbors as well as most of the shopkeepers were Italian, there was very little incentive for her to learn English. Although she would pick up the language over the years, her accent would always make her version of English—or Itanglish—somewhat indiscernible to outsiders. "BACK-eh" was back, "CAR-roe" was car, SHOOZ-eh" was shoes, and so forth. And while my mother and her brothers learned English in school, my grandmother insisted they speak Italian at home.

They remained in Goodman Place, in a spacious two-bedroom apartment overlooking the Connecticut River for about eight years. After my mother was born she and my grandfather had two more children—boys they named Corrado and Bruno. My grandfather earned a handsome salary as a stonemason and helped construct or repair a number of historic buildings in Hartford, including the state capitol. Nonni, in addition to managing and maintaining the household, took in sewing for a dollar a day. She had learned to sew from her grandmother and, by the time she was a young teenager, was an adroit seamstress.

In 1929, when the stock market crashed, there was no more stonemasonry work and the Catani's sailed back in November of 1929 with all of their hard-earned savings. Nonni Upstairs had not trusted American banks, and instead stashed their money in secret hiding places around the apartment, including under the proverbial mattress. So, while most people lost their life savings in the crash, my grandparents had lost virtually nothing except the option to remain in America.

On their return to Italy, my grandfather built a stone house for his family on the outskirts of Cortona. This small Tuscan village is about 30 miles southeast of Florence and just six miles west of the farming village, Foiano, where my father's parents originated. My mother, Tosca, only eight, fell in love with Italy.

"Italy is a country of great enchantment, romance and resplendent, landscapes," she would tell us kids. Cortona, she said, was celebrated not only for its brilliant art and stunning architecture, but also for its massive, ancient wall, built by the Etruscans to surround and fortify the town. Cortona, we learned, was also known for the Basilica di Santa Margherita, where the withered up remains of the 13th century saint were intact and on display.

"I was terrified when my mother and father took me to see her for the first time," my Mom once recalled. "The Basilica was the biggest church I had ever been in; it sits on the top of a hill and you could see the beautiful landscape of Cortona below. I lost my breath when we first entered it. It was nothing like the churches in America. It had beautiful paintings on the walls and on the ceiling; these are called frescoes. I just stood there, with my mouth open, looking all around in complete amazement, trying to take it all in. Your grandmother explained their significance, as she held my hand and we walked closer to the line of people in front by the alter. I didn't know what to expect. My mother told me that Santa Margherita died in 1297; '*so*,' I thought, '*would there be an ogre lying up there?*' As we got closer, I saw her entire body lying under glass; her skin looked shiny and rubbery, and it had a discolored, chocolaty brown look to it. I hid my face behind my mother, who chastised me for not showing reverence to this saint who had devoted her entire life to helping sick people. I told my mother I was sorry for being rude, quickly made the sign of the cross—*Nel nome del Padre, e del Figlio, e dello Spirito Santo*—and dashed toward the exit. I even forgot to bless myself with holy water as I ran out. This scared me and it made me afraid of seeing dead people."

Mommy told us that the Basilica also had special significance because the priest and nuns there saved her mother's life. Nonni was born at home, as was the custom at the time, but there were complications with the birth. No one ever explained why, but I believed it had something to do with fact that Nonni's parents were first cousins. Apparently, the blue-blooded Manciati clan had its fair share of the inbreeding that comes with nobility.

Nonni was barely breathing when her aunts cut her free from her mother's life support, wrapped her in clean, stiff white linen sheets and ran an eighth of a mile to the Basilica to baptize her before she died. Catholics believe that an unbaptised baby will not be allowed to enter into the Kingdom of Heaven but instead, would remain in Purgatory, a sort of temporal wasteland, for all eternity. But my grandmother, to the astonishment of her aunts, the nuns and the priest performing the baptism, did not die. They took it as a sign from God. They shouted, "*ché miracolo!*" *Grazie Dio, per questa angela!*" (The Nonni Upstairs I knew was hardly an angel.) As a tribute to what they believed was a miracle, the nuns named her Margherita. Her father was furious because he had chosen the name Elisa (pronounced ee-LEE-sa) for his second daughter. Although her legal name remained Margherita Elisa, he would call her Elisa or Liza, just to spite the Catholic Church. From then on, friends, family and acquaintances would know her as Elisa, or just Liza.

Every morning, before she left for school, my mother strolled with Nonni to the outdoor market to buy fresh vegetables and fish, meat or whatever looked good and was priced right that day for the midday meal. There, to my mother's delight, they visited with friends and relatives. "Franca, how's the fish today?" my grandmother would ask. "It stinks like a dead, rotting horse, Liza," Franca would respond. "But the *fettini* look pretty good." Further down the road, "Ciao, Liza! Pietro has some beautiful *asiago* today." Mom would run into some of her school mates, and they'd exchange smiles and exclaim "*ci vediamo subito*" (see you in a bit). When Nonni reached the bread shop, she always bought Mom a small piece of *ciaccia*, fried dough, lightly sprinkled with granulated sugar.

One Saturday out of every month, Nonni Upstairs took my mother and Corrado to Florence, or *Fireze*, as Mommy always uttered with great elan. Bruno was too small, so he was left in the care of my grandmother's sister, Letizia and her husband, Aldo, who lived in the stone house next door to them, also built by my grandfather. Early in the morning, my grandfather would drive them to the train station, and for the entire day they would stroll, shop, gaze at Michelangelo's David at the Galleria dell' Accademia, or visit the Galleria degli Uffizi, home to the art of Da Vinci, Michelangelo, Giotto, Botticelli, Raphael, Tiziano and Caravaggio. Built by the Medici family in 1581 to house their administrative offices, it extends from my Mom's favorite square, Piazza della Signoria, where a replica of David still stands, to the River Arno. They rarely went across the Ponte Vecchio, because back then it was filled with mainly blacksmiths and butcher stalls. My grandmother told her children, when they clamored to walk over the bridge, "We didn't come to Florence to smell bad meat and fish; we can do that in our own backyard."

Nonni Upstairs and her daughter Tosca felt their life in Italy was *la doce vita*, full of good food, friends, music and art. "*Voglio stare in Italia per sempre,*" Mommy told her mother—I want to stay in Italy forever.

We lived on Greenridge Road on the outskirts of Torrington. My father's brothers, Freddy and Livio, had built two brick, side-by-side ranch duplexes on adjacent lots that were nothing more than scrubby, dusty sand piles. It would be years before magnificent red-sugar maple trees, ones that I would climb just about every day of my life, would anchor the front yards of our homes. Only three other homes had been built on this dead-end street, which was zoned for at least another twenty-five. The homes would eventually be filled with many Italian families, including the Favali's, Mastro's, Marciano's, Vedivelli's, and the Avania's. Most were second and third generation Italians who had already been homogenized into the American culture, people who ate spaghetti from a can, chicken that was "shaked and baked," bologna sandwiches, and Swanson's frozen T.V. dinners in front of the T.V., on T.V. trays.

Nonno and Nonni Next Door lived on one side of the house and we and Nonni Upstairs on the other. In the two-family brick duplex next door to ours, Uncle Freddy and his wife Auntie Gloria lived with their two kids, Audrey and Louie. Uncle Livio's American wife, Pauline, who my family called "la Americana" and, much to the dismay of Nonni Next Door, was not Catholic, did not want to live on Greenridge Road under the thumb of her mother-in-law, so they moved into a big house closer to the center of town. They had two kids: Valorey and Georgie, who were much older than my brothers and I, and because they didn't live within the boundaries of our immediate extended family, we never got to know very well.

I much preferred the Riccucci side to my mother's, the Catani's. The Riccucci's were less inhibited. My father, for example, thought nothing of walking around our house in his baggy underpants and if the need arose, of farting. Ricci and I found this hysterically funny, especially when Daddy pointed his finger at us and let one rip. Our laughter, of course, only encouraged him. My mother was forever rebuking my father by simply saying his name, "George," in a gentle, disapproving tone. Nonni Upstairs would simply shake her head, frown and sigh.

Further annoying to my mother and Nonni Upstairs, my father, his brothers and parents, walked freely into each other's homes without knocking or even ringing a doorbell. My brothers and I were with my father on one particular occasion when he went to discuss a business matter with his oldest brother, Uncle Livio. We walked into the house and my father called out, "Livio?"

We heard my uncle's muffled voice coming from the bathroom, "In here."

My father and the three of us marched into the bathroom where my uncle was sitting in a bubble bath, shaving. He was chewing on an unlit, half-smoked, fat stinky cigar. How he could shave and smoke at the same time was mystifying. Daddy closed the toilet seat cover, sat down, and proceeded to talk business. My brothers and I blithely stood around waiting for them to finish. Ricci and I rifled through the various toiletries on the bathroom shelves and in the medicine cabinet. Johnny scolded us and said, "I'm going to tell Mommy on you two, and you're gonna get it." Johnny had inherited the Catani's sense of propriety, while Ricci and I acquired the Riccucci's free-spiritedness and I'll-do-as-I-please attitude. We looked at Johnny, giggled, made faces, and continued what we were doing.

The ancestral class differences made for some very entertaining not to mention explosive events in the contemporary lives of the Catani and Riccucci families, particularly around holidays. We always spent holidays together, either at our home, Nonno and Nonni Next Door's or at both, where everyone would go from one side of the house to the other during the course of the day. Meals were the cornerstone of Italian families, and holidays were always celebrated with elaborate foods, beverages and treats, beginning with antipasti, and ending with strong coffee and a digestivo, such as anisette, vermouth or vin santo. My grandmothers, Mom and Auntie Gloria prepared the meals.

Each holiday had a unique primo and secondo piatto. For Easter, we started with my favorite pasta, *gnocchi*, a potato-based pasta served with a meat sauce and sweet sausage and meatballs. Next, roast pork prepared with lots of garlic and with a dry herb grown and found only in Italy: *finocchio*. This herb is harvested from the finocchio plant long before its flowery tips turn into seeds, in America known as fennel. Homemade bread, a colorful salad, and several *contorni* or side dishes were standard fare at not only holiday meals, but every meal in our house. One of my favorite side dishes was fresh beets, blanched and then tossed lightly with oil, vinegar, garlic and a bit of fresh oregano and black pepper. I always knew when my Mom was making beets for dinner because her fingertips would be stained a blushed pink from having cleaned and cut the fresh beets from our garden.

Thanksgiving meant lasagna, prepared in the Toscana tradition—plenty of meat sauce, mozzarella, parmesano, and NO ricotta cheese. Instead, the Toscani used a white sauce, or *besciamella*. To celebrate our Americanhood, we ate roast turkey, prepared not American style with bread or cornmeal stuffing but with *ripiano*, a dense, beef and veal based mixture that resembled a meatloaf and was slid, uncooked, into the turkey cavity. The turkey was basted with fresh garlic, olive oil and fresh Rosemary. Ricci and I liked to watch Nonni Upstairs roast the turkey because she was very thorough and serious about roasting any kind of meat. She rotated the turkey in the roasting pan so that at any given time the bird would be resting in any number of positions including, which was the most bizarre, its side.

A few weeks before Christmas, the ravioli were prepared. Nonni Upstairs would lay out her huge cutting board, which virtually covered the entire surface of our dining room table. She carefully prepared and rolled out the pasta with her rolling pin, which was about a yard long, at least three inches in diameter, and had no handles. This enabled her to easily roll out the pasta into huge sheets. She next dropped onto the large sheets of pasta, dollops of a mixture consisting of ground chicken, ground turkey from our Thanksgiving leftovers, which had been frozen (Italians do not discard any type of food substance), spinach, veal, and various fresh herbs spaced about one-and-a-half inches apart; she would then lay another huge sheet on top. With a small wooden-handled implement that had a tiny serrated wheel at its base, she cut the ravioli into their neat, small squares. My brothers and I were always assigned the tedious task of pinching shut the four sides of each ravioli with a fork. Ricci and I hated it; John seemed to relish it. We all, however, loved the final product, which was served with a red meat sauce and sweet sausage and meatballs. A Christmas Ham and *contorni* were served after the ravioli, but no one ever seemed to eat much after having stuffed ourselves on the *primo piatto*.

My grandmothers were very confident about their culinary prowess. If anyone complimented them—*è molto buòno; speciale; migliore*— they would shrug their shoulders, not look up from their plate and sarcastically respond, "*ma che ti credi te*?" which literally means, "well, what do you think?!" and figuratively means, "like I need you to tell me this?!"

Sally and Nello often joined us on the holidays. Nello Menchini was a long-time friend of Nonno and Nonni Next Door's; they knew each other in Italy and maintained their friendship in America. Nello was my brother Ricci's baptismal godfather.

Nello was "rich," as my brothers and I would say; he bought a new Cadillac every three years. It seems that every Italian immigrant aspired to own a Cadillac, because it was a symbol of success and wealth in the new country. Nello lived in a huge modern-furnished brownstone in Hartford, where he also owned an enormous amount of property inherited from his wife after she committed suicide when she learned Nello was having an affair with his secretary, Sally Palmer. This whole affair was all hushed up and I didn't know about it until I was much older. Nonetheless, my family had an extraordinary fondness for Nello and Sally, the Americana, and treated them like family.

My brothers and I especially loved Sally; she was high-spirited, had a great, infectious laugh and often bore a thin, deep-red, glass-rim-shaped stain that curled up slightly at each side of her upper lip from all the red wine she so loved, especially that which was made by my father and grandfather. Nonni Upstairs, who thought the world of Sally, sometimes jokingly referred to her as *la ubriacca*, the drunken one. Sally always had Liberty Bell half dollars stashed in her big white patent-leather pocketbook and every time she came to visit, she'd open it up and pull out a handful for my brothers and me. And, she bought us the best Christmas gifts, except that one year when I was nine years old, she bought me a dress; I hated dresses and cried when I opened the box.

Just about every holiday was accompanied by some antics from either my Dad or Uncle Livio or Freddy. I remember one Thanksgiving when the adults were sitting around the dining-room table just before the antipasto was served. The children always sat at a "kid's table," just off the dining-room table, so as to give the adults more privacy for grownup talk. Suddenly, we heard a loud outburst of laughter coming from the grownup table, with all the Riccucci's laughing and the Catani's, including Nonni Upstairs, my mother and Uncle Bruno, smiling politely. As the youngest, I of course got up to see what was going on. My brothers always relied on my inquisitiveness and boldness and knew, as the youngest, I would get the least severe reprimands for poking my nose in places that it didn't belong.

I happened to spy a small white packet resembling a restaurant-sized pack of sugar circulating around the table. The writing on it was very tiny, so I had to get real close; when I read it, I was completely baffled; what was so funny about something called "Instant Pussy?" What did it mean? My mother scolded me for being nosy and promptly sent me back to the kid's table. When I told my brothers and cousins, Louie and Little Johnny, Uncle Bruno and Auntie Mary's son, some giggles were provoked from Louie and my brother Johnny. We called my brother Big Johnny in the presence of Little Johnny to distinguish between the two. Apparently, Big Johnny and Louie got the joke but Ricci, Little Johnny and I did not. I called them a couple of lunkheads and said I didn't care and didn't want to know anyway—so there! Louie just kept snickering and meowing at me.

I never, ever saw my mother or Nonni Upstairs in anything less than a slip. Oddly enough, growing up I knew more about the male anatomy than the female. I thought nothing of walking into rooms where my father or brothers were changing. It was no big deal, met by Ricci and me with a roaring laugh. And I didn't care who saw me naked either.

Saturday night was bath night. In those days, everyone except perhaps for WASPs, bathed only once a week. Because I was now seven years old, I wasn't allowed to bathe with Ricci anymore; this made bath night even more unforgivable. After dinner, my brothers and I each took a bath and then had a snack of a glass of cold milk and homemade cookies, brownies or chocolate pudding with crushed walnuts on top. My Mom, like my grandmothers, made *everything* from scratch, so we always had delicious chow and desserts. After our snack we settled in for Saturday night T.V.: *Laurence Welk*, Nonni Upstairs' favorite program, which I found boring except for the black tap dancer, Arthur Duncan, and the blond, ultra-exuberant piano player, Jo Ann Castle, who smiled broadly as she banged out ragtime hits. Next we watched *Hollywood Palace*, a particular favorite of us kids.

One Saturday evening, Ricci and Johnny had finished their baths and were sitting in the kitchen dunking their chocolate chip cookies in big glasses of icy cold milk. My mother was running my bath and I was standing in the bathroom buck naked, shivering, waiting to jump in the nice warm tub. Then, an idea popped into my head. "I'm going to crack Ricci up," I said to myself. I could always count on him for a laugh and we were always trying to outdo one another. So I ran out of the bathroom and into the kitchen and did a little jig for my brothers. They looked up from their snacks and began to howl hysterically, falling to the floor on their knees. Their laughter, in turn, made me laugh so hard I peed right where I was standing on the kitchen floor. A stream of warm pee shot to the floor and collected into a small yellow puddle between my feet. This made us laugh even harder. My mother came into the kitchen, shook her head and ushered me into the bathtub. I thought she would holler at me. But my mother didn't even scold me; she just mopped up the pee.

Nonni Upstairs blamed the Riccucci in me.

According to Nonni Upstairs, my father was "a country bumpkin." Whenever she referred to him in this way, I'd shoot back, "Don't you say anything bad about my daddy." He never seemed to mind the mild aspersions, but I was quick to let her know that I wouldn't tolerate them.

Growing up, I was glued to my father. I followed him around like Bebe did, from the moment he left for work in the morning until he arrived home at night. I adored him; I was a "Daddy's girl," his *bambolina* as he always called me, and his little doll was extremely jealous if he gave his attentions to anyone else. I was even jealous when I looked at the framed wedding picture of my parents, where my father's hand rested on my mother's. I hoped, like every young girl, to someday marry my father. My brothers teased me unmercifully about this.

One day, as I did every day, I waited by the picture window for my father's blue Ford pick-up truck to pull into the driveway. And it did, at 6:20 p.m. on the dot. I wanted to be, had to be, the first to greet him hello. "Daddy's home!" I yelled and then ran to him when he walked into the front door, trying to jump into his arms. Out of nowhere, Ricci came bounding and pushed me out of the way, taking my place. I started to cry and pout, and pulled Ricci from my father's arms; "you big stupid head," I told Ricci. "Daddy, you go back outside and come in again so I can hug you first," I demanded. A big smile spread across his face and without protest, he did so, just as he did every single time.

As I got older, my brothers and I would walk to the end of our short, dead-end street to meet my father driving home from work at the shoe store he owned. We stood on the corner of our road and the very busy Main Street, stretching our necks to spot his pick-up truck in the oncoming traffic. When Daddy pulled onto Greenridge Road, I would run up to his window, stand on the running board and kiss him hello; we'd then pile into the bed of the truck. Sometimes we would open the tailgate of the truck and sit on it, swinging our legs and feet off the back. Johnny once came up with a great idea. While my father was driving, we would slide our butts off the tailgate, run in back of the truck, continuing to hold onto the tailgate, and then jump back on. My father always drove extremely slowly when we sat on the tailgate but I don't think he ever knew we were jumping on and off it. It became a competition of sorts among the three of us. Once, Johnny slid off the truck, proceeded to run behind the tailgate, holding on, only he was having a hard time jumping back onto the tailgate. Ricci and I kept yelling, "jump up, Johnny; jump up." But he couldn't. The next thing you know, he was still holding onto the tailgate, but he was dragging by the knees, down the middle of the road. We could hear his dungarees scraping and grating against the pavement. Ricci and I yelled, "Let go, Johnny," and he finally did. The truck kept going, and there was Johnny lying in the middle of the road. For what seemed to be an eternity, Ricci and I froze. When Johnny got up, brushing off his jeans, and Ricci and I realized he wasn't hurt, we busted out laughing. Johnny made a face at us and walked the rest of the way home. My father never knew what had happened.

On Saturdays, I often spent the day with my father at his shoe store. Sometimes Ricci came, too. I tried to help Dad whenever I could, but typically I would spend the day trying on shoes, playing with the cash register and stamp machine, and raiding the till to run down to the corner five-and-dime, Chedester's, to browse through all the large wooden bins containing small toys and trinkets. I had an obsession for tiny, miniature objects, which I stored under my bed in a large, old round hatbox that Nonni Upstairs gave me. My collection included two squirt guns; a small Gumby, a pocket knife with a plastic blade; an official, very worn Yankees baseball; a stack of Topps' Yankees baseball cards; a plastic egg with my ball of silly putty; several Matchbox cars; a metal trick handshake buzzer; my lucky rabbit's foot—bright red—keychain; a Kazoo; compass; a cheese-cloth sack with six shiny glass cats-eye marbles and one shooter, and several No. 2 pencils sharpened down to within one inch of the eraser. No dolls; I hated them. I tried to avoid running into the eerie, stern Mrs. Chedester, who wore long black Evangelical missionary dresses, her gray hair cropped closely to her head, and those clunky, black orthopedic shoes that tied on the sides; Ricci and I called them moon boots. I often wondered if she was a man underneath that dress.

Or, I would go to Jacob's drug store, where I would sit at the counter and drink a coke or eat an ice cream cone, while twirling around and around on the bright red-leathered stool. Jacob's father, who I called "the old man" would often sit with me and ask me about school.

He was constantly making faces behind his son's back and mimicking him; I was a very receptive audience, which only further encouraged his high jinks.

The best part of the day was when my father and I ate our simple yet ample lunch packed by my mother: a meat of some sort, such as cubesteak, a vegetable, bread, and Jello sometimes with bananas or fruit cocktail suspended within the thick gel. The vegetables and Jello were always packed in large canning jars. My father had a small broiler in his stock room, where he would broil our meat. And because Jello wasn't my favorite dessert, my father always stopped at Jimmy's general store on our way in and picked us up a pack of Hostess Twinkies. I preferred Hostess Chocolate Cupcakes, but my father couldn't eat chocolate because of the ulcer he got peeling potatoes during the war. So, I always told him Twinkies were my favorite. We each ate one with our Jello.

On those Sundays that my father painted the new houses built by his brother, Uncle Livio, Ricci and I tagged along. While Daddy painted, Ricci and I ran around throughout the wall-less rooms looking for slugs, those small, round pieces of metal that were punched out of electrical junction or outlet boxes. We'd collect them and pretend they were money. Once, when we showed our cousin Louie the stash we had collected, he said, "You can use those in gumball machines; they work; I've tried it." I said, "That's cheating!" Louie responded, "Norma, it's only a gumball." It figures he would say that. Louie had shown me how to jump-start a car, inhale cigarettes, make a farting sound by cupping my hand under my armpit, hawk up the best lougies, and make crank calls. My favorite was calling the "Ed Sullivan's" in the phone book, and when Ed got on the line, I would say: "I'd like to audition for your show," and then I'd start singing a song. Most of the time Ed hung up before I'd finish. Louie was forever getting in trouble. Grown-ups in the family constantly referred to him as a "thick head" or *testa dura*. Ricci and I thought using slugs was dishonest, so we never tried it. Besides, our Dad had a gumball machine at his shoe store. I wouldn't have liked it very much if someone did that to him.

One Saturday, when I was about eight, I was playing with the cash register at my father's store, and a big, fat lady came in with her young daughter. They were black and they were both wearing very worn cloth coats. The little girl's shoes looked so old I wondered, wasn't she embarrassed to walk around in them? The woman said that her little girl needed new shoes, but that she could only spend about ten dollars. My father measured the girl's foot, asked the mother if she wanted ties or slip-ons, and what color did she have in mind.

As my father was gathering some shoes from the stock room, I came around from behind the counter where I was pretending not to be watching, and went and slouched down in the seat next to the little girl, who looked about my age. She wasn't very tall, so her feet were dangling, lightly swinging and swaying off the end of the seat; one of her very white socks had a tiny hole so I could see the tip of her pinky toe sticking out.

I said, "Hey."

She looked at me and said, "Hey."

"Buyin' some shoes?" I asked trying to think of something to say to her, and she said "yep."

She didn't seem very interested in talking to me, but I persisted. "What grade you in?"

She said, "the SEH-kent."

Just then my father returned from the stock room with about four boxes of shoes. She tried them all on, and her mother asked which ones cost ten dollars or less. My father said they were all ten.

I tried to interrupt, "No, Daddy . . ." because I knew all of those shoes were at least thirty dollars or more. I've tried on enough of those shoes to know how much they cost. I tried to correct him.

But he cut me off, and said "Honey, go see if we have any extra shoehorns in the back." I begrudgingly slid off my seat and trotted off to the back room for a shoehorn. By the time I returned, the lady was standing at the cash register paying my father for the pretty black patent-leather slip-ons. I gave him the shoehorn, which he placed in the shoebox, now holding the little girl's old, worn-out shoes. I walked over to the little girl who was admiring her new shoes in one of the floor mirrors.

I said, "Those are pretty."

She said, "I love 'em."

The black lady took her daughter's hand and walked out the door. I watched through the window as they walked away, slowly shrinking, fading into the sidewalk, until they completely disappeared. I never saw them again.

After they'd left I said, "Daddy, you made a mistake. Those shoes weren't ten dollars." And he patiently explained to me that the little girl needed shoes and her mother wasn't able to afford a good pair of shoes for her. And, I asked, "But, did you lose money on that sale?"

And he replied softly but firmly, "That's not the point; think about it for a minute."

I could only think how glad I was that fate had made him my father.

If not for the vagaries of world economies and wars, my parents, whose own parents came from villages in Tuscany not 10 miles apart, might never have met.

Though my mother and Nonni had longed to stay in Italy forever, my grandfather was unable to find steady work. If the economy was bad in America in the early 1930's it was near collapse in Italy as in other parts of the globe. In the early part of 1934, my grandfather sailed back to America in search of work. Two months later, he sent for his wife and children. My mother, just thirteen years old, was broken-hearted.

Nonno Catani assured my grandmother that they would remain in America for only a short while. My grandmother, to hedge her bet, left her middle child Corrado, now ten-years old, with her father-in-law. She reasoned that Corrado had just started school and it would be imprudent to pull him out if the family would be returning to Italy within a year or two. Corrado, who pleaded not to be left behind, soon relented when he received a shiny new bicycle as part of the bargain. Leaving her son in Italy was a decision that Nonni Upstairs would regret for the rest of her life.

My grandmother's life seemed to be playing out like some dark, Wagnerian opera: Several years after they had returned to the U.S. and just as they were making plans to return to Italy my grandfather died of a brain aneurysm. It was 1939 and my grandmother was only forty-two years old. She said, "Nothing good comes from living in A-MAAH-ree-cah, A-MAAH-ree-cah."

Her first inclination was to work, save money and return to Italy. To do so, she fell back on a skill that was ever marketable, albeit at low wages—sewing.

My grandmother and my mother, now 18 years-old and also a proficient seamstress, began working fifteen-hour days for $2 a day at Cooperman's sweatshop in Hartford making women's dresses. Not unlike all of the textile mills in the U.S. at the time, it employed only immigrant women, who showed up for work every morning with their well-scrubbed faces, rosy cheeks, worn hands and cloth coats. Cooperman's employed mostly Italian women, but there were also some Polish, or poe-LOCK-ee, as my grandmother called them. My grandmother's youngest son, Bruno, now fourteen-years-old, was studying to be a photographer. He helped very little with Nonni and my mother's goal of returning to Italy.

Nonni and Mom's hopes of returning to Italy soon vanished as the United States unexpectedly entered into World War II. It was too risky to set sail for Italy and besides, Italy was an Axis nation, at war with America. She continued to work in the sweatshop, saving her hard-earned money. My mother became a Rosie-the-Riveter welder at Pratt and Whitney in Hartford, Connecticut, and much to the dismay of her mother, wore overalls to work.

For city life, Hartford wasn't so bad. It wasn't *Firenze* or *Milano*, my mother said, but it was as the capitol, the hub of fast-paced, urban living and it was *the* place to shop in Connecticut, home to one of the major department stores in the region, G. Fox and Company. Hartford also housed the Bushnell Theater, which ran operas, musicals, plays and other shows at affordable prices. Outside of New York's Metropolitan Opera, it was the only theater for opera in the region. As the years passed, my mother would see many operas there. And, New York City was only a two-hour train ride away. At twenty-two, her mother now permitted Mom to go with girlfriends to New York. One Saturday of every month, they visited museums, saw off-Broadway shows in the standing-room only section, or shopped at Macy's and Gimbles Department Stores. She had always wanted to see an opera at the Met, but couldn't afford it; once the war was over, all women lost their jobs at Pratt and Witney to make room for the returning servicemen. So, my mother started sewing again at Cooperman's sweatshop, earning not even a quarter of what she earned as a welder.

Nonni Upstairs was impatient for her only daughter to marry. Tosca had been proposed to three times by a man named Frank Tavernese, but kept turning him down. Nonni was disappointed and frustrated. Frank was the son of one of Nonni's best friends, Delle, and was very refined and cultured.

Years later, when we were all visiting Delle and her son, Nonni said to me, "This is the Frank I told you about; the one your mother could have married." I looked the man up and down and said quite resolutely, "I'm glad my mother didn't marry you. My father is much better than you." My father stretched his fingers over his smile, and everyone laughed but Nonni, who grinned and squeezed a hunk of skin from my spindly upper arm between her thumb and forefinger and gave it a good twist.

At twenty-two, mother didn't date much, and her mother was growing more and more concerned. Many of her girlfriends were marrying, but my mother was in no rush. She told her mother that she was waiting to fall in love, like *La Boheme's* Mimì did with Rodolfo. "*Mama*, she would say, "*Aspetto l'uomo giusto.*" I'm waiting for the right man.

One Sunday afternoon at the Connecticut shore my mother saw my father. They had met before, fifteen years earlier when they were young kids at Sound View, a small beach resort of Long Island Sound in Connecticut that Italian immigrants and their families flocked to just about every Sunday. Sound View was just one of many beaches on the Old Lyme Shoreline, which was demarcated by ethnic divisions; Sound View for Italians, Old Colony for the Jewish, Point Of Woods for the Irish. Further up the road were the beaches of Old Saybrook. They were for white people. My Dad once told us that Katherine Hepburn and her family lived in the borough of Fenwick, Old Saybrook, in a grand, stately mansion. He said that "the Hepburns were hoity toity WASPS who didn't want to associate with riffraff Italians like us." "How sad," I thought. "Doesn't everyone wish they were Italian?"

At the base of Sound View was Michigan Avenue where the street was lined with concession stands, selling *scaciatta* (Sicilian pies filled with spinach, sausage, fried potatoes and onions), fried dough ladled with a rich marinara sauce and topped with a heavy dusting of Romano cheese, and what became known as Italian Ice, which, Nonni Upstairs said, really wasn't Italian at all. The Sicilians had something called *Granita*, which was made of ice, sugar and flavoring. But according to my grandmother, that wasn't Italian at all; it was Sicilian, which isn't Italian according to my grandmother. This didn't stop her from slurping down a few of her favorite, lemon, ices during the day.

My father loved to tell us "when I saw your mother sunning herself on the beach that day, my head spun. I plopped down on the sand beside her and started chatting her up." I blushed when he said, "she had a great figure, too. She was wearing a tight one-piece black bathing suit, and I kept asking her to go for a swim with me, but she wouldn't. She didn't want to muss her beautiful long hair," at which point he would strike a coquettish pose and caress an imaginary heap of long hair on his head.

From the old black and white photos, I had the perfect image of my mother and dad from that time. My mother was a cross between a slender young brunette Barbara Stanwyck and Joan Crawford. She had a light, creamy complexion with long, curly hair and beautifully big dark eyes. She had an enormous wardrobe, because she and my grandmother, with the exception of shoes and hats, made all her clothes. My mother sported different dresses, skirts, blouses, hats, gloves and open-toed, close-toed or spectator shoes, in each photo. She had a beautiful, slender figure, and an arresting pose, as if her photo were being taken for a fashion magazine. My father was a strikingly handsome George Brent, particularly when he grew his thin black mustache. He was a snappy dresser, too. I only knew him to wear his signature bow ties every day. But, back then, he wore jazzy, splashy ties, with full-cut trousers, and dapper loose fitting jackets, either double-breasted or the more couture for the late 1940s, single-breasted with pronounced shoulders, notched lapels and three buttons. He wore lace-up bucks or wingtip, spectator shoes, and in some photos, he wore a smart, wide-brimmed fedora.

Very soon into their courtship, Nonni Upstairs, forever bold and audacious and also dismayed that her 28-year-old daughter was not yet married, asked my father what his intentions were. *"Che sono le sue intenzioni con la mia figlia?"*

My parents were married in November of 1949. Although my mother wanted to live in Hartford, my father urged her to live in the small factory town of Torrington, 30 miles outside Hartford. "It's only for a few years, Tosca," he assured her. Nonni Upstairs would be living with them. "A package deal," Nonni Next Door exclaimed sarcastically.

Our house and my grandparents' were adjoined in front by an enclosed breezeway, so we scooted back and forth between the two sides many times throughout the course of a day without having to go outdoors. And, just about every morning I, along with Ricci and sometimes Johnny, ate breakfast there. As we sat perched on our knees on her large dark Walnut dining room chairs, Nonni Next Door would boil Medaglia D'Oro espresso in a small pan and then strain it into big bowls for us. She added lots of Carnation evaporated milk and stirred in about three teaspoons of sugar. If she was making bread that day, she would fry us some *ciaccia,* fried dough, and sprinkle granulated sugar on the top. Or we ate small homemade breads or *panini*, homemade *biscotti*, or some plain old American Royal Milk Crackers, which we would crumble up into our bowls of hot coffee. Nonno would be long gone by this time either hunting in the deeply wooded area which began just beyond our massive garden, or toiling with Nonni Upstairs in the garden where we grew all sorts of vegetables and fruits, from sumptuous plum tomatoes to fresh, crispy *finocchio* (fennel). We even had a small grape vineyard. Every two years or so, my grandfather and father pressed the dark purple grapes to make red wine. I was one of their helpers and loved the intoxicating smell of mushed grapes, alcohol, and the wine soaked wooden barrels that filled our wine cellar. I also got to test the final products.

As my brothers and I ate our breakfast, Nonni Next Door would be puttering around the kitchen, gesturing with her hands, telling us about her life in Italy, funny stories about Nonno, or just spinning some of her usual tales which invariably had a moral to them. She had an indefatigable sense of humor and was physically demonstrative; even a simple facial or hand gesture—which invariably accompanied any utterance from an Italian—made me laugh. She had an ability to mix words in the Italian language that inevitably made me and anyone else around explode with laughter. It was very typical, for example, for her to announce in her classic high-spirited way to family members or friends who contradicted her, "*Siete tutti* FULL-eh SHIT-eh" in her customary part Italian, part Itanglish way.

Nonni Next Door had a penchant for cursing. And somehow it was okay because the Italian language is so flowery and elegant that Americans couldn't decipher what was really being said. She could call someone a shithead, yet it rolled off her tongue in such a way that the "*catsone*" would think it complimentary.

I kept a constant, adoring gaze on her. Nonni was a very stout, robust woman, whose height about equaled her girth. I loved trying to wrap my skinny little arms around her. Nonni Next Door had an inexplicable quality that made me feel very safe. Her large breasts particularly fascinated me because they were the first I had ever seen, naked that is. One evening around 8 p.m., we were watching Green Acres on T.V. when the telephone on my grandparents' side of the house started ringing. It kept ringing and ringing and finally my father got off the sofa and walked next door to answer it. Ricci and I followed him. I don't remember who was on the other end of the phone, but after a few minutes, I saw my grandparents who were still half asleep walking toward the phone asking "*chi è?*"—who is it? Ricci and I just stood there paralyzed, mouths agape. Nonni Next Door was wearing her thin knee-length granny panties with no top and Nonno wore a tank-top tee shirt with no bottoms. I didn't even notice Nonno but my eyes were glued to Nonni Next Door's chest. I had never seen women's boobs before and these were humongous. It didn't seem to faze my father one bit. Before long, my mother was behind Ricci and I ushering us back to our side of the house. "Mommy, her *petti* are huge," I exclaimed.

"Just keep walking," my mother whispered.

Nonno and Nonni Next Door often took us for Sunday drives in their dark-blue, hardtop 1957 Cadillac Eldorado Seville. Their sons had bought it for them, and it symbolized my grandparents' pride for their sons and the prosperity of being successful immigrants in America. I loved this big shinny car and was especially fascinated by its front bumpers—protruding, black stumps of hard rubber that came to a point; they looked like miniature torpedoes. Ricci said they looked like ladies' *petti*, or boobies.

There were also what I called "kids' seats" in the front and the back of the car; they folded down and before I grew so tall, were the perfect size for my small butt. Johnny liked to correct me, "They're arm rests, dummy." Naturally, as "the baby," I sat up front with my grandparents. Sometimes, there was no particular destination in mind; other times, we would drive into to the country to pick fresh berries, with which Nonni Next Door would bake wonderful fruit tarts or *crostate*, with almond flour to give it a nutty flavor and perfectly shaped criss-crossed strips across the top to form a lattice pattern. I loved the long aimless road trips and how fast Nonno drove. I think every Italian has a predilection to speed, and my grandfather was no exception. I encouraged Nonno, telling him to fly, "*vole, vole, voliamo.*" My grandfather said "Americans don't know how to drive, and they drive too slowly." As he passed all the cars along the way, he told us that in Italy, there weren't paved highways; and most of the streets were still dirt. But Italians still drove fast, even though they had no place to go.

Nonni Next Door would bark at him, as she stretched her rather generous arm across my lap, to slow down, our grandchildren are in the car ("*andare più lento, i nostri nipoti sono nell'machina*"!) Nonno would say something like, "*Maria, mi rompe i mei coliogni*" (Maria, you're busting my balls). "*Stai zitta, o ti metti nel'*TRRRUN-coh" (And, if you don't shut up, I'm going to stick you in the trunk). This always provoked giggles from my brothers and me. So, too, would my grandmother's very curt retort: "*vaffanculo,*" which means, depending on the circumstances, "up your ass," or affectionately, "oh, go fuck yourself." I think in this case, Nonni meant both.

Nonni Next Door and Nonni Upstairs did not get along. Both strong women, they were nonetheless cut from different cloth.

My father had been born and raised in the small town of Winstead, Connecticut, where his parents had emigrated from Foiano, not far from Cortona. But the Riccucci's and Catani's never knew each other in Italy.

Nonno and Nonni Next Door landed on Ellis Island on April 4th, 1914, with about forty U.S. dollars they had borrowed from family and friends in Italy. Unlike Nonni Upstairs, Nonni Next Door wanted to come to America, especially since after she married Nonno she had no choice but to follow Italian tradition and move in with her in-laws. My grandmother, who was much too independent, free-spirited and outspoken to live with her in-laws, proclaimed, "No house is big enough for me and my mother-in-law!" They packed their bags and off they all sailed to America. My grandfather was twenty-four years old, my grandmother twenty-one.

Nonno was a laborer. He didn't build houses, but he worked at the Tiffany Lumber Yard in Winstead, cutting, lifting and moving lumber for fifteen hours a day at the rate of two dollars per day. Within two years he found a better-paying job in nearby Torrington at the American Brass Mill, which manufactured brass pipes and similar sundry parts. My grandfather worked most of his life on the factory assembly line there, except for a short stint as a bricklayer. My grandmother, like most immigrant women, also had a full-time job taking care of the house and family.

Despite my grandfather's cawing and strutting, Nonni Next Door was the defacto ruler of the Riccucci roost. She liked to refer to herself as Maria Cencini Riccucci, but everyone called her "*La Maria*," or The Mary. This short, rotund woman was, as Nonni Upstairs would later call her, the "*BIG-ah boss-ah.*"

Nonni and Nonni lived in a small, one-bedroom, third-story flat; they had three sons: Livio, in 1914, Alfredo, who was called Freddy, in 1916, and my father, Giorgio, in 1917. The Riccucci's truly lived the American dream: my grandfather worked hard and saved his money; and all three of his children were entrepreneurial and would build up a small empire of businesses and property that enabled the entire Riccucci family to ultimately live a comfortable life. But, it didn't come easy. While they all had dreams of going on to college, none of the Riccucci sons were able to finish school because they had to work and help support the family. Livio had to quit school after 8th grade, Freddy barely made it out of elementary school and my father dropped out of high school during his first year. They all took an assortment of odd jobs or worked in American Brass alongside their father to earn money and help support the family. With the strong work ethic instilled in them by their parents, they invested their earnings in land, which ultimately enabled them to develop lucrative trades.

Livio became a contractor and with his brothers as business partners, built homes throughout Torrington. Uncle Freddy and my father, with Livio as their business partner, owned shoe stores, "Riccucci's Shoes." Uncle Freddy was actually more a shoe cobbler, cleaning and repairing. His inventory was also much smaller and narrower than my father's. While my father sold every type of shoe imaginable, Uncle Freddy sold mostly men's work shoes—those ugly, clunky black or dark brown tie shoes that working-class men wore with dirty white socks. I always believed that my uncle became a cobbler because of his own physical impairment: he was what they called "lame" back then and had to wear a Frankenstein boot on the foot of his short leg to elevate him to near equilibrium. Despite the fact that differences were accentuated and pitied back then, it became such a familiarity to my brothers and me that we were never really conscious of his bum leg.

Uncle Freddy's store had a three-person, shoe-shining bench that we loved. One had to step up to sit down, and then rest one's shoes on brass stands shaped like the bottom or soles of a shoe. When we had our dress shoes on, we were forever shining shoes for each other.

My father's shoe store was in the North End of Torrington. This was the working-class section of town where one would expect to find working-class shoes. But my father, whose tastes ran to the more refined, sold high quality shoes of all styles at affordable prices. Even businessmen bought their wingtips, loafers and oxfords from my father. He also had the best selection of Ked's sneakers, which, aside from my Sunday shoes—black or white patent leather slip-ons-is all I wore growing up.

I once asked Nonni Next Door, "Aren't you proud of Daddy, Uncle Livio and Uncle Freddy?" But, as was typical for her—and maybe Italians in general—she was apprehensive about expressing euphoria or pride. Anger, surprise, sadness could all be binged on with archetypical bellowing and cacophonous Italian melodrama. But not happiness. Perhaps it had something to do with old Italian folklore that one shouldn't be too happy about anything, because if you are, it will be taken away from you. Or maybe it was the familiar domestic martyrdom of a Catholic matriarch. In any case, Nonni masked her happiness and responded to my question by waving her hand in the air, slightly crinkling one side of her mouth, and after a short pause, emitting a vapid, monotonic, whine, almost like a feline purr-cry: *"eh."*

Religion and God played a crucial role in our family. Neither my grandparents nor my parents were what you might call evangelical Roman Catholics, the ones who had a small, pastel-colored, plaster-of-Paris statue of the Virgin Mary standing in an upright bathtub on the front lawn. But, just about every room in our house had a crucifix hanging in it, sometimes with rosary beads draped around the dying Jesus' neck. And both my grandparents and parents had one of those miniature pink plastic figurines of the Madonna affixed, with a magnet, to their car dashboards. It was symbolic, reverent and very Italian. With the exception of Nonno and Nonni Next Door, all of us went to church every Sunday, on holidays and on any other holy day of obligation.

Nonno and Nonni Next Door sought salvation and grace in their own unique way: they were forever inviting the priests and nuns from our local parish, St. Peter's, to our house. The nuns were invited to get fresh fruits and vegetables from our garden. The priests, unlike the nuns, were often invited to dinner because Nonno and Nonni Next Door wanted to keep in their good favor; the priests were their tickets to heaven, their indulgences, they professed. I remember one occasion when Father Salvatore joined us for dinner. Father Sal, as we called him, was the family's favorite parish priest, mainly because he was old-world Italian. When my mother called out that dinner was ready, I ran to the table and immediately reached, before even sitting down, for that scrumptious-looking antipasto—a huge platter of prosciutto, salami cotto, cappacolo, soppressata, mortadella, provolone, big hunks of asiago and Parmigiano Reggiano, marinated articoke hearts, roasted sweet peppers in olive oil, mammoth black and green olives and a red-leaf lettuce garnish. My older brother Johnny clipped me in midstream and whispered reproachingly, through clenched teeth, "grace." We never said grace in our home but I knew better to question it with Father Sal sitting at the head of the table. Father Sal instructed "It is customary for the youngest person sitting at the table to recite grace." I slowly turned my gaze away from that antipasto, looked up at Father Sal, and said rather chagrinly, "I don't know grace." I could feel my face burning from the blood rushing to my head. I wasn't embarrassed for myself, but rather for my parents. I could imagine Father Sal admonishing them, "What kind of parents are you, that your own daughter doesn't know how to recite grace?" But when I glanced over at my mother and father, they both had very loving, sympathetic smiles on their faces. Ricci was giggling and Johnny, whose obsequiousness I deplored, sneered at me in a gloating, pious manner and blurted out, "I'll say grace." And he did, during which I let out, without even lifting a cheek, a silent but very noxious fart.

The nuns were never invited to dinner at our house because to Nonno and Nonni Next Door, they were at the very lowest rung of the paradisiacal and ecclesiastical hierarchy. In other words, they couldn't be much help to them. I myself felt great ambivalence towards them; they were forever rebuking me, beating me up during my catechism classes for talking. Catholic children are required to attend weekly catechism classes, I am now convinced, in order to drill into our heads that good people go to heaven and live peacefully when they die, and bad people burn in hell.

With their "clicker" noise makers, they would wander around the room, cloaked in dark, mysterious black habits, ever fashionable in the 1960s, with only their craggy, ashened-old faces poking out of those hard white coifs, which kept them well-armored, obedient and in a constant state of emotional, physical and no doubt libidinous distress. Hands coupled behind their backs, they were forever clicking those cricket noise makers at us to be quiet, stay still, or pay attention. Once, because I was clicked several times for talking too much, Sister Zita forced me to go outdoors, pull my skirt up and kneel, with my bare knees, for one solid hour, on the concrete steps of St. Peter's school. Every now and then, she would glare at me through the window with her pinched face, shaking her index finger. I thought, "you old battleaxe."

And yet, I pitied them, too. They were forced to drive around in old, rusty, broken-down station wagons, had to wear those heavy, oppressive liturgical vestments, were prohibited from presiding over Sunday Mass, and had to take a vow of poverty. The priests, by contrast, drove around in Cadillacs, wore whatever they damn well pleased, providing they wore one of those sacerdotal, stiff, white, detachable collars, were sole chieftains of Sunday services, and had the nuns, not to mention the young altar boys, waiting on them hand and foot. Although I didn't realize how insignificant it was at the time, I thought I was contributing immensely to the nuns' welfare by clipping food coupons for them; they'd redeemed the coupons for their face value, worth about 1/16th of a cent.

After the priests and nuns left, Nonni Upstairs made a wisecrack remark under her breath about how insightful Dante Alighieri was in his classic allegorical masterpiece, *La Divina Commedia*, whose *peregrinatio*, or journey of hardships, described a series of spiritual tests and life lessons. She explained how Dante assigned the souls or "shades" of priests, popes and other historical and mythical figures to fitting slopes of hell for divine retribution for their earthly sins. For Nonni upstairs, one of Dante's most clever *contrappassi* was that of Popes Nicholas III, Boniface VIII and Clement V, who were all stuffed head first into holes resembling baptismal fonts. Only the baptism involved not the moistening of their heads with holy water but the torturing and burning of their "soles" with oil and fire. Nonni said this was just and fitting retaliation for their abuse and misuse of their office. They're all a bunch of *bugiardi* (liars), *imbroglioni* (cheats) and "CROOK-ee" (crooks).

I seemed to recognize, even back then, that there was nothing ethereal or inscrutable about the pope, priests or nuns. Nonni Next Door once told me that "*sono delle persone come noi*" (they are people just like everyone else).

The feuding between my grandmothers started almost immediately after my parents married and moved to the house in Torrington. In Italian families, it is the mother, in our case, grandmother, who is the locus of power, not the father, or grandfather. And my two grandmothers were *so* Italian in their altercations.

One day Nonni Upstairs planted a small rose bush in our front yard. She tended it carefully, watering and patting the earth around it. That night, Nonni Next Door snuck out in the middle of the night, pulled the bush up by its roots and threw it across the lawn. The next week, when Nonni Next Door planted something, Nonni Upstairs uprooted it. No words were exchanged between the two, only a lot of ranting and raving behind each others' backs: "*porca miseria*" (damn it <u>or</u>, miserable sow/ swine, take your pick); "*accidente quella stregga*"(damn that witch); "*non mi freggare*" (she's not going to screw me), and other choice phrases that, because of their inflection and intonation, never failed to made me laugh convulsively. This, before I understood that the strains which drove them to conflict, could one day hurt me, too.

My mother was the consummate conciliator, who always intervened and made things right. She did so first by giving birth to a son, Johnny, at which point the battling between my grandmothers went underground. My mother may have been a diplomat, but also stronger than my father, who, for a Riccucci, was reserved and somewhat deferential. As the baby, his mother coddled him especially since he would be the last of her children. Rummaging through her dresser one day, I found a round, butter cookie tin filled with faded sepia toned photos. In one, my father was wearing a dress! When I ran to my father with it, asking why he was dressed like a girl, he said, "back then, all young boys wore dresses because it made it easier for potty training, and it was cheaper; as I grew, my mother just kept letting the dress out so it would fit." If anyone else had given me that explanation, I wouldn't have believed it.

My father, in turn, doted on his mother, and treated Nonni Next Door like a Queen. If Nonni Upstairs wasn't calling her the "*BIG-ah boss-ah*," she was calling her "*La Regina dell' bosco*," the queen of the woods, since she saw Torrington, compared to Hartford, as a hick town.

Act I. Scene 2.
Ore Dolci e Divine

("*Happy, Golden Hours*," from
Puccini's *La Rondine*)

My mother and Nonni Upstairs may have been happier in Italy, but I loved our life in Torrington.

Every year on August 15th, my father organized a parade for the neighborhood kids. This day marked Ferragosto, an Italian holiday, once a celebration marking the end of a long summer laboring in the fields, now a feast day and Holy Day of Obligation by the Catholic Church. Everyone dressed up in a costume, and Johnny led the parade in our bright yellow, four-wheeled, surrey with the red and white candy-striped, fringed vinyl top we got one year for Christmas. Kids with plastic masks of Top Cat, Casper the Friendly Ghost, Heckle or Jeckle—one or the other, I could never distinguish between the two—Felix the Cat and other cartoon characters marched behind Johnny in a single file. My mother dressed us in brightly colored costumes every year. The costumes often had an opera motif— the clowns, *Pagliacci*; the Chinese ministers to the princess in *Turnadot*, Ping, Pang and Pong, complete with large Chinese straw hats. One year I was a Geisha for *Madama Butterfly*; my mother put white pancake makeup all over my face and hands and loosely wrapped a scarf around my calves so I could only take small, shuffling steps. My brothers were so jealous; they asked our mother if they, too, could be Geisha girls and she said, "Why not?"

My father followed the procession in his pickup, which Johnny decorated as a float with big blue and purple-passion Hydrangea from our yard and flowing lavender crepe paper. Ricci and I sat in the back on folding lawn chairs, throwing out candy to the kids too young to participate, like Peggy O'Brien. I always felt sorry for Peggy; her Mom wouldn't allow her to march in our parades so I'd throw her one of the real good candies—a fat Tootsie Roll, a Chunky, Bit-O-Honeys, a box of candy cigarettes, an O'Henry bar or a small pack of Nik L Nip Wax Bottles filled with sweet rainbow colored juices. Our neighbors lined both sides of the street, clapping and waving as we passed by. Even my mother and grandmothers stood to watch as my father honked his horn and tipped his Pork Pie hat to them; Ricci and I giggled, smiled and screamed out "Mommy, catch the Chiclets!" One of us threw her a box of peppermint, her favorite.

Although my mother was more genteel and reserved than my father, she was a good sport. Like the time she was learning how to drive. When she lived in Hartford, there was no need for her to drive; it was a big city so she took the bus everywhere. But in suburban Torrington, my mother eventually realized that she would need a car to go shopping, run errands, pick us up after school, take us to the movies. So when she was about 38 years old, my father gave her driving lessons.

On her first driving lesson, we all packed in our maroon Oldsmobile Super 88, Mommy at the steering wheel, my father sitting next to her. In a family that did everything together, it never occurred to my brothers or me that we would be excluded. I hopped in the front seat next to my father; this was a given—no matter how old I grew to be, I was "the baby" in the family and thus had the right of first refusal to the front seat, next to, or in between my parents; my brothers jumped into the back. My poor mother was jerking that car, accelerating and then slamming on the brakes, all the way down our narrow, dead-end street amidst giggles and laughter from my brothers and me. She never scolded us; she only let out the occasional nervous laugh. I kept saying, "Mommy, don't slam on the brakes so hard." My father, trying to keep a straight face, added the occasional snicker as well. To make matters worse, I somehow managed to mention the driving lesson to some neighbors the previous day, and so several people, adults and children, lined the street to watch my poor mother lurching and jolting the Super 88 to the end of our road. They cheered her on: "Go Tosca, you can do it!"

My mother was not fond of camping, but every summer she took my brothers and me to Hammonasett State Park in Madison, Connecticut, on Long Island Sound. My father bought a used, slightly faded silver and pink twenty-seven foot trailer that had one small master bedroom at one end, with a tiny shower that he never hooked up, and a nifty dinette at the other end that converted into a double bed. My brothers slept there, while I slept with my mother, except on Saturdays and Sundays, when my father was with us. He came down on Saturday nights after he closed his shoe store and stayed until early Monday morning. Those nights, I slept in a sleeping bag on the floor just beside their bed. We also had a galley kitchen with a small refrigerator and gas stove; my mother cooked pasta with different sauces every night, and Johnny would grill hot dogs, hamburgers or sweet Italian sausages for afterwards.

We went to the beach every day. My Mom, since the Sundays she spent at Sound View, loved the shore. She relaxed on a folding, aluminum beach lounge chair under an umbrella reading or listening to our AM transistor radio. Johnny often sat under the umbrella with her trying to stay out of the sun. Ricci and I would laugh at him, lying on the beach blanket covered in towels and wearing one of my Mom's big straw sun hats. My Mom slathered us with Coppertone, so we wouldn't get sunburned.

Ricci and I spent most of the day in the water, making sand castles, or taking turns burying each other in sand up to our necks. We loved it when our Mom came swimming with us. She wore a one piece black bathing suit, not too tight, and always crammed her hair into a white bathing cap with a strap that went around her neck and snapped on the other side. She once tried to get me to wear one, but I refused, protesting that "I'm not walking around looking like a Q-tip in that thing!"

Ricci and I liked to dig for muscles by the rock jetties jutting out into the ocean. We would collect a bucket for crabbing. Later in the day, Ricci and I rode our bikes throughout the camp grounds, stopping at one of walkways over the multitude of streams that winded through Hammonasett. We'd pry open one of the half-croaked muscles with a sharp rock, then tie a piece of the heavy string—that my Mom used to truss chickens for roasting—around the side cradling the blob of slimy, sunflower-yellow meat. We'd then drop it into the stream waiting patiently for a crab to scurry along the bottom with its large pincers to take the bait. Mostly they were Lady Crabs, the kind non-Italians used to make crab cakes. When we spotted a crab nibbling voraciously at the muscle, we'd slowly pull up the line one fist over another, and just as it neared the base of the walkway, we'd jerk the string firmly to free the tenacious crab. We liked the sport of crabbing but never thought of them as edible. Plus, as creepy as they looked, we couldn't stand the thought of hurting one. My Mom once asked, "Why don't you bring a bucket of crabs back and I'll fixed us a nice pasta sauce?" But Ricci and I said we'd rather starve than eat one of those disgusting, *vomito* crustations.

My Mom, who always wanted to learn how to ride a bike, had her wish come true at Hammonasett. She rode a big, hunter-green second-hand bike with thick tires that my Dad picked up at a thrift shop. As he would for any beginner, my Dad fitted the bike with large training wheels. My Mom rode that bike so proudly with my brothers and I by her side; Johnny on his shiny, brand new Raleigh Sports English 3-speed Bicycle, Ricci riding his unicycle, and I at the helm of the tandem bike my Dad built for us from two second-hand bikes and painted black and orange tiger stripes by Johnny. Our fellow campers, turning to stare and point, seemed nonplussed, undoubtedly trying to figure out if we were with the Zoppé, that famous Italian family circus. If Nonni Upstairs could see us, she'd admonish my Mom, "Tosca, *ma sei matta?*" (Are you crazy) running around like a gypsy?

Although Mom appreciated the relaxation of being at the shore, there was one thing she absolutely hated: no indoor plumbing. We had to use the outhouse, *il cesso*—literally, the shithouse—or, as my brothers and I fondly referred to, the honey-bucket. It was a small wooden room, about 3 1/2 by 4 feet wide and 6 1/2 feet high; it had a small little screened-in window at the very top to air out the stink. It had a wooden, enclosed bench with a hole in it. My father outfitted the hole with a plain white toilet seat so as to prevent ass splinters. Some campers put plaques on the outside of the door, like "home sweet home." I wanted to put up a "Riccucci" sign or a half moon, but my mother said no, because she didn't like anything adorning or drawing attention to the *cesso*.

Sometimes, when she was in there doing her business and I spotted the sewage trucks coming into view, Ricci and I would run to the honey-bucket and yell, "Mommy, the honey-bucket men are coming." Within seconds, she would be running back towards the trailer, and we burst into giggles. We always hoped to see toilet paper hanging from the back of her bathing suit or sundress, but this never happened.

It made Ricci and I sick to think of those guys who came along in those huge green trucks emptying the buckets. They were always young guys sweating like pigs in heavy brown overalls, wearing thick gloves and surgical masks over the bottom half of their faces. One guy would swing open the little trap door behind the outhouse at its base, pull out a metal pail filled with poo and pee, hand it to someone standing on top of the truck, who dumped it in a hole, sprayed the empty bucket with a pink solution that smelled like Clorox, handed it back to the other guy, who replaced it behind the trap door. "Yuk," we always thought, "who would do such a job?"

My mother stuck out the camping for my brothers and me as well as for my father who also really loved it. When he arrived on Saturday night, he went for a swim, no matter how late. Ricci and I joined him, even though the water was dark and cold. Johnny stayed in the trailer, reading; my mother would sit on a towel on the cold, damp sand watching us the entire time. As Ricci and I were taking turns diving off my father's shoulders, she'd yell out, "Be careful. George, don't let them get hurt." We'd wave at her to let her know we were all right. I can still see her small hand waving back at us.

The year Santa Claus brought me a drum set, my mother was not very excited. I was eight years old and in 4th grade. I'll never forget waking up Christmas morning, running into the living room and finding that sparkling Slingerlands, blue-crystal trap drum set, complete with a base drum, snare, cymbals, tom-tom, high-hat and floor tom-tom. I screamed out, "a drum set," and ran to it and began pounding away. My father beamed with delight. My mother was sitting quietly on the sofa smiling, but clearly she would have preferred something more demure, such as a flute. Yet she seemed proud of my ability to keep a beat. And she didn't object when I practiced diligently in the months that followed.

That August, as we did every year, we went to the *festa* at the Knights of Columbus Hall in Manchester. It was sponsored by *La Società Toscana*, a social club whose members were immigrants from Toscana and had settled into various towns and cities in Connecticut. It was held on the Sunday closest to Ferragosto.

After Sunday mass in our respective Roman Catholic churches, everyone congregated at the big grange-like hall. It had several rooms—the largest of which was for eating and then dancing—outdoor *bocce* courts, and separate rooms with pinball machines and pool tables. Outside the hall was a long bar that was never in operation for the *festas*. It had shinny chrome beer and soda spigots and several faucets, sinks and bar stools. The younger kids like myself played a made-up game we called "bar." We'd take turns playing bartender and the customers smoked candy cigarettes and belted down shot glasses full of water. "Gimme another," we'd yell out to the bartender.

We also liked watching the old men play *bocce*. They wore their undershirts, old hats, drank red wine, and chomped on those crooked little stinkweed Italian cigars. I had already learned how to play a good game of *bocce* from these old men. The trick was to sneak down the *bocce* court as far as possible before releasing the ball. You knew it was time to release it when the opponents and onlookers started jeering, waving their hands in the air, giving the *mal' occhio*, the evil eye, while snake-hissing, and yelling obscenities in Italian: "*Catsone, lanciare la palla*"—Shithead, throw the ball!

Around noon, we sat down to eat. Long tables filled the hall and on each of them were large loaves of Italian bread, carafes of red wine, and small dishes of celery sticks and black olives. First we ate from giant platters of antipasto scattered around the tables. Next, we ate pasta, the *primo piatto*. This year it was rigatoni in red meat sauce, with meatballs and hot and sweet sausage. Next came the *secondo piatto*: roasted chicken with *contorni*—roasted potatoes and *cicoria* (dandelion) sauteed in olive oil and lots of garlic. Last came coffee, which we kids drank too, and dessert, which was invariably spumoni. All the while, the middle-aged waitresses buzzed around the room in their hairnets, black uniforms and efficient white shoes. The old Italian men, including Nonno, would flirt with them.

After dinner, the tables were cleared and removed from the hall. It was a respite for our mothers, grandmothers, and aunts because it meant no cooking or cleaning. Once the floor was cleared, the band set up on stage. The band consisted of a piano player, drummer, bass guitarist and, of course, an accordion player. The band played mostly Italian polkas and couples whirled across the floor smiling and laughing. My paternal grandparents especially liked to dance, and would sometimes clear the dance floor as they gracefully—notwithstanding Nonni Next Door's wide circumference—swept around the hall. Ricci and I always got a good giggle at the old ladies dancing with one another; they had the most serious, deliberating looks on their faces. I thought, "*Why aren't they dancing with men?*"

This year, the band took a break and my Dad asked the band leader, "Could my kids play a couple of songs on your instruments?" I loved this about my father: Don't be afraid to ask for something if you really want it; the worst that could happen is that someone will say no. I was not shy, and bold was an understatement. So, I immediately ran on stage and picked up the drumsticks.

Johnny whined, "I'm not going up there to play in front of everybody." Johnny took piano lessons, but he didn't have the self-confidence to play for an audience.

I said, "Why not?"

Johnny said, "I'm too embarrassed. And what if I make a mistake?"

I replied, "Johnny, you won't flub up and so what if you do. Who cares?"

He said, "Everyone will laugh."

"Johnny," I said, "don't think of people as being mean; they won't laugh. And if they do, who gives a flying crap. They're not worth it." He just walked away.

Ricci joined me on the stage and sat behind the piano. We played a bunch of contemporary tunes like "96 Tears," "Wipeout," and a rocked-up version of "Heart and Soul." Much to our amazement, all the young people, aged 16 to 25 or so, bolted to the floor and started dancing. Even my cousin Audrey was dancing the Twist or the Swim. For me, this was the ultimate compliment.

Audrey, My Uncle Freddy and Aunt Gloria's girl, was my very favorite cousin. She was eight years older than I and had the best sense of humor. She indulged me in my clowning and acted in-kind. Like me, she was a prankster. She was also one of the prettiest girls I'd ever seen. She had big beautiful olive-shaped eyes, a long Modigliani-esk neck, and long, straight sandy brown hair that she usually teased up into a Bouffant; she must have used four cans of Aqua Net hairspray to keep it lacquered to her head. She dressed like the girls on "77 Sunset Strip," the ones that Kookie dated: tight Capri pants and body-hugging sleeveless, short-cropped tops. She was so cool. She even took me for long rides in her convertible, powder blue, three-on-the-floor Ford Falcon with white bucket seats. Before I got in, she asked, "Norma, are your hands clean?"

I chortled, "Yep, they're clean, Audrey."

"How about your shoes? Did you wash them before you got in?" She questioned with a sly smile.

"Well," I fibbed, "I did step in some dry dog poop, but I'll scrape it off on your dashboard," as we both snickered. The AM radio would always be blasting with something cool: Frankie Vallie and the Four Seasons, "Let's Hang On (To What We've Got)"; the Supremes, "Stop! In the Name of Love"; Lesley Gore's, "It's My Party."

I was so excited now to see all these people dancing to our music. So, too, was my Mom. Beaming proudly, she had tears streaming down her face. She even ran up to the stage and yelled, "These are my kids playing."

When it was time for us to stop, the old-fashioned Italian band started to play and my Dad, who loved to dance, began to make the rounds. First he danced with his mother, then my mother, then his mother's widowed friends and then others. This time, he waltzed Auntie Gloria, who couldn't dance much with Uncle Freddy because he was lame. She was a great dancer, too. I didn't think she could ever do anything wrong.

I idolized my Auntie Gloria; she was my favorite aunt and she used to tell me "Your Mother is like a sister to me." They shared secrets, she said, and could commiserate about living under the reign of their mother-in-law, Nonni Next Door. She was tall, thin and had beautiful, snowy-white hair. She told me it was "prematurely white," whatever that meant. All I knew was that she looked super and I liked being with her. She treated me like a young adult, and didn't patronize me as though I was some little kid. She was very special and extraordinary, especially for a girl: not only did she know how to drive a car, but she could also drive our three-on-the column blue Ford pick-up truck and the three-on-the-floor Scout Jeep, jointly owned by my Dad and Uncle Freddy. In the days when automatic transmission was the latest craze, most women never learned how to operate vehicles with manual transmissions. She was so amazing. If I weren't spending time with Nonni Next Door, I'd be with Auntie Gloria, riding with her in the Jeep to run errands for Uncle Freddy or going grocery shopping at the A & P, where she'd buy me a pack of Hostess cupcakes or a cherry Hostess Fruit Pie. Sometimes I would eat dinner at her house because I liked to watch her cook and I loved the American meals she prepared: fried chicken; corn bread; macaroni and cheese, and the best coleslaw I ever tasted.

After Auntie Gloria sat down, my mother danced one or two more times with my dad then found her friends from Hartford, whom she saw less of now that she was living in Torrington, to catch up on old business.

The next time I turned around, my Dad was dancing with a lady in a very short black dress that had long fringes attached to an extremely low-cut collar. The fringes draped over her rather generous, pointy breasts. She wore sheer black stockings and black satin spike heels. She was a good dancer. I didn't know her name, but I knew she was a widow.

I was furious, not to mention hysterically jealous. I marched onto the dance floor, right up to them and yelled over the accordion player, "Mommy wants to dance with you, Daddy," a lie at best.

He said something like, "O.K., after this dance."

I persisted, pulling at his arm "But she wants to dance now!" The lady with the fringes smiled at me, all the while her huge boobs were bouncing and swaying, about to smack me in the head. Fortunately for my Dad, the song ended, and I was able to drag him from the dance floor.

Soon enough, he realized my mother was nowhere to be seen. Eyeing the widow, I felt panic rising inside of me.

"Why don't you dance with Nonni Upstairs now?"

He looked at me and squeezed my cheek. "She doesn't dance."

I darted around to find Nonni Upstairs at a table at the edge of the hall. She was with her old chums from Hartford and they were playing cards. First gin rummy, now *scopa*.

Interrupting her card game, I said, "Daddy wants to dance with you."

"No, piccolina, my back is hurting," she said. "Besides, I'm on a winning streak. Go play with your brothers and stop pestering me."

As we were driving home, I made my father promise never, ever to dance with the lady with the fringes again.

"Should I worry, George?" my mother asked with a laugh.

"Never," he said, patting her cheek with his hand.

The year after my debut as a drummer, my father came home one night with a cheap clarinet that he'd picked up from a shoe salesman selling him new footwear. My mother was delighted. Even more than my Mom, my Dad took a strong liking to the instrument. He hired an acquaintance to give me lessons and sprawled out on my bed to hear me practice after supper every night, his stocking feet tapping away into blank space. I practiced the scales and songs I learned, but always ended my repertoire with "I Left My Heart in San Francisco," a particular favorite of my father's, who would invariably be snoozing when I finished.

The clarinet solved another problem. When I was taking drum classes at school, I was the only girl; it didn't seem to make a difference to the teacher or the boys in class, or so I thought at the time. But, when we began rehearsing in April for the Memorial Day parade, the music teacher informed me, "You can't play the drums in the band. You'll be playing the cymbals." I looked up at him, my forehead furled, and asked, "Why can't I play the drums? I'm the best drummer you have!" He said, "I know that, Norma, but girls shouldn't be playing the drums in public." I shot back, "What are you talking about? Why can't I?" He just shook his head and bellowed, "You play the cymbals or you don't play at all." I yelled at his back as he was walking away, "Well why did you let me take drum lessons in the first place?"

I was so outraged; I carped about this to my mother who said, "Go to the school principal and complain; don't ever let anyone tell you that you can't do something because you're a girl." My mother told me to fight for what I wanted. I remember what she told me when I said I wanted to be a baseball player when I grew up. I loved Mickey Mantle and Roger Marris and it was my dream to someday play for the New York Yankees.

"But, there aren't any girls on any of the baseball teams," I once observed to my mother.

She said, "You could be the first. If you really want to do something in life, do it, and don't let anyone tell you that you can't."

The next day, I argued with the music teacher but he wouldn't budge. Because I wasn't a quitter, I played the cymbals in the Memorial Day parade. Although I continued to play drums and would go on to take private lessons, I dropped out of the school band but not before telling the music teacher what he could do with his drumsticks.

One year, for Halloween, we were the Beatles. I was Ringo of course, Johnny was John, Ricci was Paul and my father was George. Nonni Upstairs and my mother made our costumes. They used black yarn for our hair and we set out in search of loot, leaving my Mom to answer the door at our house. We always saved Mrs. Crane's house for last. "Can't we skip this house, Daddy?" I would request with a moan. "No, honey, it's not neighborly; just be nice and smile, okay?" Mrs. Crane was an old, somewhat loony woman, who had a bad memory, stale breath and never seemed to comb her shoulder-length, thin, grey straggly hair. We called her the candy-corn lady because every year she would come to the door with this huge, beautiful sterling silver bowl of loose candy corn; she would thrust her hand in the bowl, grab a handful, and drop it into our paper Halloween bags. We waited patiently, as candy corn tinkled and trickled down our bags, pinging as they hit bottom. She showed a crooked, affective smile, and would say, "Lovely costumes" over and over again. We threw out the candy corn when we got home.

As was our custom after trick or treating, all of us from the neighborhood—Ricci, Johnny, me, Robbie Favali, Jimmy O'Brien, Louie and Christine Mastro—went out to soap widows, TP people's houses or knock on front doors and run. We hid behind bushes and laughed when the person opened the door and no one was there. Johnny watched, but didn't participate, saying "It's not nice to play tricks on our neighbors."

"Johnny, that's the whole point of the 'trick' in trick-or-treating; only we're greedy; we want the tricks *and* the treats." Everyone laughed.

At the end of the night, Louie put me up to knocking on Mr. Panko's door. He was a dour, scary curmudgeon that we all feared. Louie once told us, "Mr. Panko killed his dog by hitting it over the head with a shovel; its eyeballs fell right out of its head." Like a dope, I believed him. Needless to say, no one ever went looking for treats at his house. Besides, a few days before Halloween, he'd tack a cardboard sign with big block letters on his front door, which read: "**DO NOT KNOCK ON MY DOOR!**"

I quietly crept up to the side of his house and knocked on a window. I inadvertently knocked so hard, my hand went right through the small windowpane. Everyone heard the crash, and we all lit out, running in different directions. I was so scared; I started running home, calling out for Ricci. I caught up with him.

"You cut your hand?"

I hadn't even noticed the tiny drops of blood trickling down from my middle knuckle.

"Let's go to cellar so I can wash it off." We snuck into the cellar through the door from our backyard, so our parents wouldn't catch us. My knuckle was barely scratched, didn't even need a band aid. As we were roller-skating to Diana Ross and the Supremes' "Baby Love" in the cellar, we heard a big ruckus upstairs. The cops, who we called "the pigs" back then, showed up at our front door with Johnny in tow. Apparently, after we all scattered, Johnny, instead of running home to tell our parents, went to hide at the house of our friend, Joni Marciano, who wasn't with us that night because she was straightening her hair. He told her what had happened and asked, "Wanna see what Norma did to Mr. Panko's window? Come on, I'll show you." As they were sneaking around the back of his house, they saw a cop car with its red lights flashing and a couple of pigs talking to Mr. Panko. Before they could scurry away, one of pigs spotted Johnny and barked out, "Hey, you! Get over here." Instead of running, my obedient, respectful brother walked over to him and the pig very abruptly grabbed him by the shoulder. Johnny screamed like a girl then yelled, "I didn't do anything! It was my sister."

He escorted Johnny to our house, and I could barely hear what my parents were saying to him: "Just kids" . . . "playing" . . . "an accident" . . . "no harm done" and the worst, "We'll pay for the broken window." Then "good kids" . . . "sorry" . . . "goodnight, officer."

I slouched down in one of the heavy walnut chairs at our big kitchen table with my head hunched over, waiting for the ax to drop. I was beginning to realize that my fears were greatly misplaced, because the impending ax never seemed to drop. What I really feared was hurting and disappointing my parents. This would become a far greater threat and deterrent than the prospect of a good chewing out.

Ricci sat with me calmly saying, "It'll be okay, Norma." He was more frightened than I. Johnny ran into the kitchen and screamed at me, "You got me in trouble, you retard." Neither my mother nor my father scolded me; they knew they didn't need to. They could see that I felt like crap for the shame I brought them. My mother asked, "Did you hurt yourself, *Normina*?" I said, "No, I'm okay, Mommy." I slunk to the bathroom, washed up, got into bed, and waited for my mother to come into my room and sit beside me where she'd talk to me as she did every night. Johnny and I had switched bedrooms at this point, because I was too old to sleep with Ricci.

"Did you say your prayers?" Mom asked tonight, as she did every night.

"Uh huh" I responded, smiling and waiting for her to tickle me. Then, she bent over to kiss me and I wrapped my skinny arms tightly around her neck, pulled her close to my face, kissed her cheek and whispered in her ear, "I love you Mommy and I'm sorry. Leave the hall light on for me, okay?"

"I love you too, *Normina*. Sweet dreams."

That night, I woke up in the middle of the night. The darkness frightened me and I tiptoed towards my parent's bedroom, thinking I could sneak in their bed with them while they were sleeping as I had so many times when I was younger.

My mother softly called out my name, "*Normina*?"

"Mommy, I can't sleep."

Then, without waiting for a response, I ran and jumped in bed, between my Mom and Dad. I slid into a safe, warm sleep.

The first time I was denied something I really wanted began with my mother sitting me down and telling me, "I'm taking Johnny to the opera."

Why Johnny? Didn't she know I was the one who loved opera? And to take Johnny! Sometimes I secretly wished that it was Johnny who'd get yelled at instead of me; I wished Nonni Upstairs would give him *uno schiaffo in testa*—a slap in the head. But he was such a goody two-shoes he never seemed to get in trouble.

I was a scrappy, tomboy, so self-confident and tough I'd often defend my older brother against bullies. I was tall enough to do it. Throughout grade school I towered over all the girls and most of the boys. I hated dresses, dolls, and curled hair. And except for school and church, where dresses were mandatory, my mother never forced me to wear skirts or dresses; I wore dungarees, tee shirts and Ked's sneakers. My knees were forever scraped and scabbed from sliding into bases on our blacktop street where we played baseball nearly every day except in the winter months. Nonni Upstairs liked to remind me that "*si sono vestiti elegantemente*"—your parents dressed so elegantly. She'd then remark, "*lei si veste come un contadino*"—you on the other hand, dress like a farmer.

My mother, by contrast, always let me be the person I was, though I don't think she ever knew how tough I really was. How I would beat kids up if they picked on my brothers or me. I never hit them, but would grab them by the arm, twirl them and fling them. I think my best fling was when this one kid called my brother Johnny a sissy. I sent him flying about ten feet. He didn't get hurt, but ran off crying. And he never called Johnny a sissy again.

My mother, who had longed so much for a daughter and was herself so feminine and refined, never really enjoyed the benefit of having a little girl. But the opera. That was one love we shared. Now my mother sat with me on our red leather-upholstered rocking chair in the living room, where we often cuddled at night as we watched television. She wrapped her arms around me and said, "Honey, when I was twelve, my mother took me to see my very first opera. We saw *La Boheme* at La Scala in Milano."

"Is that like the Met?" I asked.

"Yes, but it's a bit smaller."

"I wanna see *Norma*," I said.

"We'll see *Norma*. You know, Johnny is the oldest, so it's time for him to see his first opera." Her voice was tender.

I shot back immediately, "but I wanna go, too."

"Honey, now you have to wait your turn," Mom said patiently and delicately.

Then, I put my right hand over my chest, just above the heart, and said, teary-eyed, "but the hole."

She only smiled sadly. "Normina, I'm taking Johnny to the opera this time."

They had tickets to see Verdi's *Aida*, which was one of my least favorite. But Johnny never said a word; didn't even sneer at me. I thought, "Mommy must have talked to him and told him to shut his clam hole."

Around 7:30 the following Saturday morning, my father was to drive my mother and Johnny to the train station in Hartford before going to his shoe store. I was still brooding, so when my mother tiptoed into my bedroom to kiss me goodbye, I pretended I was asleep. Then, when I heard the front door close, I jumped up from my bed and raced outside to my mother in my pj's and bare feet.

"Normina, what are you doing out here in your pajamas and without your slippers?"

"I just wanted to tell you I love you and have a good time." I wrapped my arms tightly around her waist and buried my head in her chest. I tilted my head up to her face and she had a tear in her eye. She bent down, kissed me on my forehead and said, "I love you, too. And remember, when you're 12, I'll take you, too."

My mother was listening to *Norma* on our Hi-Fi. I was playing baseball outside with Ricci, Louie, Robbie and Jimmy and ran into the house out of breath, sweating, uttering, "*Devo fare la pee-pee.*" Before dashing to the bathroom, I looked over at my mother, who was sitting so peacefully on our red leather-upholstered rocking chair. Nonni Upstairs was sitting in her chair—one of the sofa's matching pale green olive damask armchairs situated just beside the picture window tacitly designated as hers—knitting a cotton sweater-vest for my father, singing the words to the beautiful duet, "*Mira o Norma.*" She looked up at me when I came through the door and said in Italian, "You know, if your mother didn't hear *Norma* just before you were born, your name would have been Mimì."

I knew the story. When my mother was twelve, her mother had taken her to see her first opera at La Scala in *Milano.* They took a train from Florence one Saturday morning; first class. At noontime, they made their way to the dining car, where they were served a four-course meal. My mother said she felt like "*una principessa!*" Although she was accustomed to large midday meals, always presented in her Mom's favorite china on crisply ironed linen tablecloths, she liked being pampered and served by the tall thin waiters, dressed in black slacks and neatly pressed white cotton shirts. She was amazed that they were able to keep the food from spilling on their uniforms, given how the train rocked and swayed as it barreled across the Italian countryside.

When they arrived at the central station in *Milano,* they took a short cab ride to the Piazza della Scala, directly across from the opera house. My mother said the outside was nothing to look at but inside was fantastical. It had a rich red velvety interior and was framed in bright gilded stucco. There was a vaulted ceiling with hundreds of pit-stalls, four tiers of boxes and two galleries that formed a horseshoe around the stage. She said they sat in a third-tier pit-stall on the left wing and had a perfect view of the stage. They saw Puccini's *La Boheme* that day, which would become my mother's favorite. My mother was mesmerized by the music, romance and drama. She was enchanted by the love between Rodolfo and Mimì and was completely suffused in Rodolfo's desperation from the death of his beloved Mimì from consumption.

I turned to Nonni Upstairs and shrugged. "I like the name Norma better. Besides," I told her, "everyone would have mispronounced it, calling me 'MEE-me' instead of 'me-MEE,' which is much prettier and much less ordinary. I would have been really mad at Daddy if I got stuck with that name."

Nonni Upstairs laughed and started singing the lyrics from the beginning, only she altered the words to tease and annoy me. She sang, *"Mira, o Norma, a' tuoi ginocchi, son tanti sporchi . . . ."* to refer to Norma, looking not at her beautiful children on their knees, as the lyrics actually read, but rather to Norma, the one with the obnoxiously dirty knees. Granted, my skinny little knees were grimy, scabby and grass-stained from sliding into bases, but I was not amused.

It was a secret between me, my mother and Nonni that I liked opera. I'd never admit to it at the time for fear of being ridiculed by the other kids in our neighborhood. It was, after all, a bunch of women wailing at high-pitched levels, saying incomprehensible things in Italian. But the music was so very moving and entrancing, even hypnotic.

It was as though I could actually *feel* the music pumping through my spirit and soul.

Despite my ability to speak and understand Italian, I could never quite make out what was being said in an aria. I had once asked my grandmother to tell me what the lyrics actually were to "*Mira, o Norma.*" She refused, explaining in Italian, "The true meaning of opera is in the music, not the lyrics. Oh, yes, the lyrics can be beautiful and very directed, but usually the dialogue in opera is trite and nonsensical. Puccini's beautiful aria '*Mi Chiamiano Mimì*,' from your mother's favorite, *La Boheme*, begins with 'Yes, they call me Mimì. But my name is really Lucia.' Pffft. Who cares that her name is Lucia and that they call her Mimì?! This is why it is the composer like Puccini, Verdi, or Rossini who gets all the credit for opera. Who remembers the names of the lyricists?" she said quite matter-of-factly.

But I was adamant. I wanted to know the lyrics to "*Mira, o Norma.*" Yes, the music was captivating, but this could not, I thought, lessen the importance or beauty of the lyrics. Words were important to me. I was an avid reader, especially for facts and Archie comic books, which I savored over after mass one Sunday a month when my Dad bought me the latest monthly edition from Jimmy's general store. I was up to the D's in the set of Collins' Encyclopedias that my father bought secondhand from one of his customers (he no doubt swapped a pair of new shoes for the set). So, I knew that the written word could be as powerful as the spoken word—sometimes even more so.

So when I returned to the living room from the bathroom, I asked my mother, "Mommy, what are the lyrics to '*Mira, o Norma*'"? She started the record over, sat down on the rocking chair, pulled me down on her lap, and put her arms around me, as she softly enunciated the words. With her eyes closed and her head resting against the back of rocking chair, she looked ethereal. There was a glow in her face and for a single moment, with the music playing in the background, I could feel her rapture.

Più lusinghe, ah, più speranza
presso a morte un cor non ha.

Even as she said the words in English, the lyrics still eluded me:

"'A heart near death has no illusions, no hope,' Norma sings to her handmaiden, Adalgisia."

"But, what does it mean, Mommy?" I asked.
Very softly, she spoke. "Let's hope you'll never know."

Act II. Scene 1.
Solenne in Quest'ora

("*Solemn in this Hour*," from
Verdi's *La forza del Destino*")

Nonni Next Door loved to shop.

Every day, she asked my grandfather to drive her to the stores in downtown Torrington. Maybe this was her way of going to the market every day, as she did growing up in Italy. It was a small downtown area with only a handful of small shops and boutiques. The one big department store was Mertz, where Nonni Next Door did most of her shopping. She strolled around in that store for hours, looking at and touching everything; she rarely bought anything, unless my brothers and I were with her. She would let us buy pencils, pads, coloring books and crayons, but nothing frivolous. Ricci and I loved going with her because one of the highlights was riding in the old, manual Otis Company elevator. It was a very small, musty-smelling elevator with chestnut brown paneling. It could hold about four people, including the skinny old man, with no teeth and a navy-blue captain's hat who operated it. The elevator had big brass doors and a brass gate that opened behind them. The elevator man sat on his little fold-down wooden stool and made a big deal about cranking the control handle and wooden wheel to get us up and down from floor to floor—there were only two and a half floors, including the mezzanine, and the elevator didn't stop there. He indulged us for a while, taking us up and down as long as no one was waiting for the elevator, but then got sick of us giggling so much and gave us the boot.

One day while we were shopping at Mertz, I was poking in a very careful, deliberate way through huge bins full of miniature objects—plastic beer mug charms, tiny bottles and boxes, pens, pencils and the like. This day, I just couldn't seem to make up my mind what I wanted. Nonni didn't allow us to buy "JUN-keh," so I tried to stick with the practical. My grandmother was getting very impatient with me, and when I finally picked something, a tiny pen no longer than one-and-a-half inches long, she looked at it disapprovingly, grimaced, waved her hand in the air and said:

Gira, gira, gira e dopo casca una merda.

You turn, turn, turn (looking and looking for something), and then what falls (what you end up with) is a piece of shit.

This aspersion made me laugh so hysterically that I dropped the pen and made it to the ladies room just in time.

The salesladies all knew and loved my grandmother, even though she shopped but didn't buy. They often jokingly remarked that my grandmother was at Mertz so much that she would probably die there. And, she did.

She was in the lobby, by herself that day, about to leave the store and suffered a massive stroke. She was a big woman and so she must have hit the ground pretty hard. A young woman entering the store witnessed her collapsing and ran into the store screaming for someone to call an ambulance. She ran back to my grandmother, removed Nonni's gold chain with the Virgin Mary medallion and placed it in my grandmother's hand; she enfolded my grandmother's rather limp, but still warm, meaty hand around it. She gently placed her ear against Nonni's chest but heard nothing but the sounds of cars revving their engines in the otherwise quiet streets of downtown Torrington.

I will always remember that day because my Dad came home crying. I had never seen my Dad cry before or look so grief-stricken. It was about 3:30 in the afternoon. Ricci and I were sitting at the kitchen table with our coloring books and huge box of Crayola crayons and the sight of him entering the doorway and crying so frightened us that we began running down the basement stairs in an apparent effort to hide in the cellar, as if this would protect us from some unknown, yet cataclysmic event. "What was he doing home so early?" I thought. He never ever closed his shoe store before 6 p.m. Maybe he's sick.

My Dad cried out, "My mother's dead." Ricci and I ran back upstairs relieved that my father wasn't sick but not quite able to comprehend the death of Nonni Next Door. It was our first experience with death; I was nine years old. My father was completely distraught—he just walked around and around the house bawling, my mother with her arms around him, following and consoling him with every step. At one point he went into my bedroom, laid down on my bed and began weeping into my pillow. My Mom laid next to him, holding him and whispering his name through her tears, "George." I stood in the doorway crying, frightened to see my Dad in such a state.

If it hadn't been for Mom, my father would have spiraled downward into a deep, depressed state over his mother's death.

My father never talked about his service in World War II and whenever I asked him what he did during the war, he responded, "peeled potatoes." I wouldn't learn until I was an adult that my Dad was drafted into the Army as a private first-class infantryman on May 11, 1942. He was twenty-four years old. Among other things, he was assigned the job of driving heavy equipment. Because he was Italian, he was not stationed in Italy, but in Northern France where, other than one of the battles fought on the Rhine, he spent most of the war. Because of my father's reticence, I didn't know much about his early war experiences. But, I eventually came to learn where he was on June 6, 1944.

My Dad was among the troops that landed on Omaha Beach as the final Allied campaign began at Normandy. He fought with the 677th Port Company, 382nd Port Battalion. No one in my family seemed to know any of the details of the horrors he encountered because back then combat missions weren't very transparent. Photographs weren't plastered throughout the news or newspapers, and it was unheard of to show a documentary detailing the vivid scenes of soldiers getting their heads blown off. I wouldn't fully comprehend how Dad suffered until I saw the 1998 Spielberg movie, "Saving Private Ryan." The intensity of the opening footage where the Germans brutally slaughtered and maimed thousands of unwitting

American soldiers as they rolled out of their landing barges was excruciating. It was nearly unbearable to think that my father witnessed this human carnage that so captured the essence of the D-Day battle. My Dad, I thought, was one of the lucky ones who came away with his body intact. Looking back on it, though, his body may have been, but his life wasn't. He completed his tour of duty in September of 1945, but returned home a broken man in spirit, mind and soul.

My Dad was admitted to the VA Hospital in Rocky Hill, Connecticut, where he spent the next several months. No one spoke of post-traumatic stress disorder back then, because the norms and mores of society precluded such emasculate conventions for big, strong men who defended our country. They just called it a nervous breakdown. The sight of such human suffering must have tortured his gentle soul, and his life would forever be altered by his experiences on Omaha Beach.

Nonni Next Door's death seemed to affect Ricci and me in the same manner. While my Mom led Dad out of his saddened state, Ricci and I seemed to develop this pathological fear of disease and dying. If a fly landed on us, we would no doubt contract malaria; if a blind person crossed our path, we feared going blind; if we cut or even scratched ourselves anywhere on our bodies, we watched carefully, several times during the day for signs of infection; if we bumped and bruised ourselves, and the bruise began to turn that milky green that it inevitably will, it was gangrene, and amputation would be necessary.

It seemed to be quite humorous to Johnny, who exacerbated our fears with statements like, "You might need to go the doctor; it might be polio." Sometimes, for added drama, he would run to the medicine cabinet for the *medicina di prete*, the medicine of the priests, a deep, black greasy salve that came in a small tin that my grandparents brought from Italy and smelled like rotting, decaying manure. Italians believed it was a panacea, using it for everything from poison ivy to stiff ligaments. We developed an abnormal fear of going to the doctor, the purveyor of sickness and death, and we just couldn't shake it.

Mom and Dad's wedding

The grandmothers competing for best-dressed
at Mom and Dad's wedding

Norma, Ricci and Johnny cooling off on a summer's day

Christmas morning with our new surrey

Cape Cod

Hammonasett Beach

Easter Sunday, April 1961

Ricci, Mom, Auntie Gloria and me

Robbie and I, with Bebe standing

Nonno and Nonni Next Door's 50th wedding anniversary.
Standing from left, John Cassidy with his wife, my
cousin Valorey and their baby, Becky, Uncle Livio,
Auntie Pauline, Georgie, Louie, Audrey, Auntie Gloria,
Uncle Freddy, Mom, me, Dad, Johnny and Ricci.

Act II. Scene 2.
Un di Felice

(*"A Happy Day,"* from Verdi's *La Traviata*)

I had carefully painted Ricci's fingernails that day with pink and red nail polish alternately on every nail, both hands.

Until I was about seven, Ricci and I slept together in the big double bed next to Nonni Upstairs. Johnny, being the eldest had his own room on the first floor, just across from my parents' bedroom. Every night Ricci and I would giggle and whisper to each other—about Nonni Next Door with her dress all scrunched up in her butt crack; Mrs. O'Brien lecturing us on the proper use of seatbelts, even though no one used them in the 1960s; Johnny sitting at Nonni Upstairs' vanity table, putting makeup on his face. That night we were under the covers and I was inspecting each of Ricci's tiny, painted fingernails with my miniature flashlight. I got it free with 100 Bazooka Joe bubblegum comics and ten cents. I was forever saving those little waxy wrappers; each featured a comic with Joe, Mort, Herman, Pesty, L'il Pat and the rest of the gang; had a incomprehensible fortune written on the bottom and a picture of a little toy you could send away for with a certain number of comics and five to fifteen cents depending on the size of the toy. Mom showed me how to carefully tape the coins to a blank index card so that they wouldn't fall through the envelope. Johnny and Ricci didn't couldn't be bothered with collecting the comics, so they gave me theirs, which I horded. Over the years I amassed a bunch of neat toys and gadgets, like a fake cigarette lighter, whose tiny bulb illuminated, resembling a burning flame. Or, a faux silver I.D. bracelet that I could keep un-inscribed since I wasn't planning to ever have a boyfriend.

We were still gigging when Ricci suddenly plunged his thumb into his mouth. I whispered, "When are you going to stop sucking your thumb, Ricci? Only babies suck their thumbs." He gurgled through his soggy thumb, "Tastes good." He then instantaneously plucked his mushy thumb from his mouth, shoved it in my face, and asked, "Wanna taste?" I slapped his hand away, yelled, "Yuck," and we proceeded to laugh hysterically. At which point, the bedside table lamp flicked on, Nonni Upstairs sat up in her bed, brandishing a hairbrush, shouting at us to "*State zitti e andate a dormire o vi do una botta*" (shut up and go to sleep or I'll give you a smack in the head). We laid on our sides, facing each other and giggled a bit more, as I watched Ricci, with his sweet elfin head, his closely cropped, jet black hair, fall asleep holding his small stuffed red teddy bear, sucking his thumb.

Every day after school, Ricci and I went out to play by ourselves or with other kids who lived on Greenridge Road. We'd ride our bikes, two-wheeled red scooters, or skateboards, and play tag, "Simon Says," hopscotch, basketball, baseball or climb trees. And we were always competing or "dickering" as my Mom called it. "I can run faster than you, Ricci," or "I'm better at basketball," I would shout out at him. And Ricci would fire back, "You are not; I can beat you any day." (I always beat him at running, and was always the first kid picked for basketball, football, kickball or baseball.) Or, I would say, "I'm taller than you, Ricci." We were forever going up to Mom or Dad, standing with our backs together, shoulder to shoulder, stretching our skinny, lanky bodies as high as we could while standing flat in our bare feet—we never stood on our tippy toes; that was cheating—and I'd always be the first to blurt out, "I'm taller than Ricci, aren't I?" The response was always "the same," from Mom or Dad.

Ricci did beat me one time; it was hilarious to us, but repugnant, even scatological to Johnny. One day I was sitting in the living room after school, watching Woody Woodpecker. Ricci came into the living room, and said, "Norma." I looked up at him and he summoned me with his index finger to follow him. I thought, "What's he up to now?" I followed him into the bathroom, and there lying neatly on one square of two-ply, pink toilet paper on the rim of the bathtub was a brown log, about the circumference and length of one of my Uncle Livio's fat, stinky cigars. I fell to the ground with uncontrollable laughter. Johnny came running in to see what we were laughing at, and at the sight of that fat turd, went running to my mother, yelling, "Mommy, Ricci did a *cachi* on a piece of toilet paper and it's sitting on the bathtub."

My Mom walked in and said, "What are the two of you up to now?" She saw that turd, shook her head, and said, "What am I going to do with you two?" She obviously wasn't impressed by that perfectly sculpted piece of shit. Ricci and I never stopped laughing, even as Mommy picked it up and flushed it down the toilet.

Every day over the next few days, I tried as best I could to get a bigger turd on a piece of toilet paper. But, I could only muster up a dairy-queen dippity-do swirl, which made Ricci howl, and even though I couldn't outdo him, it gave me a hoot, too.

Ricci was "a-fraidy cat," as I called him. Mostly, he was afraid of little piddly stuff: getting his pants caught in his bike chain; losing his milk money; hooking a worm on a fishing rod; losing his roller skate key; kissing girls. Nonni Upstairs' theory—and she had one for everything—was that Ricci's fears stemmed from either his hospitalization at the early age of 18 months for a hernia operation, or being born at home during the great Torrington flood of 1955, which prevented my Mom from reaching the hospital after her water broke. Either or both could be the cause, Nonni said in her definitive, emphatic way. Growing up, one of Ricci's many fears was getting lost. Even if he was with my parents, he had this pathological fear of getting or being lost, especially on car trips.

I can remember the times when my Mom drove Nonni upstairs and us kids to shop in downtown Hartford at G. Fox and the big discount department store, Korvettes. I particularly liked Korvettes, which had escalators with bright sky blue and gold-stripped handrails. My Mom would take us to lunch there, at the "luncheonette." I always ordered fried chicken, and waited for the waitress to bring my Mom and Nonni their coffee with cream, which came in tiny, little bottles resembling regular milk bottles; they even had the cardboard top. I got one from each of them and would chug it down and then save the bottles to add to my collection of small doodads.

After shopping and lunch, we would visit one or more of my mother's and grandmother's vast friends from the old days at Goodman Place: Concetta, Eugenia, Vittoria, Dora and others. Some of my mother's old friends had never married, and I once made the mistake of jokingly referring to them as "old maids." When Nonni heard me say this, she gave my hair a good yank, and said through her clenched teeth, "*Sta ferma*," (keep still).

We always congregated around the kitchen table, where coffee and homemade biscotti and other treats were served. In those days, the biscotti were not chocolate, pistachio, lemon, hazelnut or chocolate dipped. They were plain except for the Anisette, which was added to the mix just before they were double-baked to a toasty golden brown.

My grandmother and a few of the other women added several splashes of Anisette to their piping hot black coffee. Unlike my brothers, I never refused a small cordial of Anisette. I would sip it slowly, savoring the strong licorice flavor, while nibbling as many biscotti my mother allowed me to eat without appearing piggy or *sfacciata*.

On these trips to Hartford, Nonni sat in the front seat with my Mom, and my brothers and I in the back. Dad rarely joined us on these excursions, even if we went on a Sunday, his day off, because he was too restless to shop or sit and visit, so he said. Mom would adventurously try new routes into Hartford and invariably get lost. A wrong turn here, a wrong turn there and the next thing you know, we'd be lost.

Ricci stood up and poked his little head into the front seat and asked, his voice trembling, "Mommy, are we lost?"

She answered in her soft, reassuring way, "Yes, Ricci, we're lost."

"Is it going to be okay, Mommy?" he asked.

And my mother, whose patience seemed endless, gently said, "Yes, Ricci, it's going to be okay."

Of course, I never missed an opportunity to be a bratty wisenheimer, so I turned to Ricci and said in a dire, urgent tone, "Oh, no; we're lost; I hope we'll find our way home. What'll we do for food? And, we may run out of gas; what's going to happen to us if we run out of gas?"

Ricci was in a state of absolute panic. Again, his little head peered into the front seat, his voice quivering, "Mommy, are we going to run out of gas?"

"No, Ricci, we won't run out of gas; the tank is nearly full," Mom assured him.

My grandmother, without even turning her head toward the back seat, bellowed, "*stregga, voi camminare*" (witch, do you want to get out and walk)? Johnny, looking out the window this entire time, turned his gaze to me and smirked. He loved it when either Ricci or I "got it."

ACT II. SCENE 3.
LA MAMMA MORTA

(*"My Mother is Dead,"* from
Giordano's *Andrea Chénier*)

It was February 1968.

Eleven years old and in the 6th grade, I walked home from school that day because Mom had some errands to run. I didn't have any homework, so I went directly into the living room without having changed out of my school clothes, turned on the Woody Woodpecker show, and flopped down on the sofa. Woody was one of my favorite cartoon characters because of his screwball antics, of which I emulated whenever the opportunity arose. No sooner had I sprawled out my lanky, long body than Nonni Upstairs walked into the living room.

I expected Nonni to ball me out for lying on the sofa in my school clothes, but instead she went and sat in her chair and started crying. My stomach dropped and I felt the blood drain from my face. While Nonni Upstairs was very emotive in the quintessential Italian sense—bellowing laughter, fury or commands with the proverbial waving of the hands in the air—she only cried when something was terribly wrong. I jolted up from the sofa. "What's wrong, Nonni?" She responded in Italian, "*la sua mamma deve andare all'ospedale.*" My stomach dropped further.

"Why does she have to go to the hospital?" Nonni didn't respond; she just sat there in her chair and cried. Maybe my mother was sick because after all, she was old; she was 46, which seemed ancient from my perspective at the time. But, she hadn't looked sick or acted sick. I felt very scared and wished instantly for Ricci. But he was in junior high school now, riding home on the bus and wouldn't be here for at least another hour.

Whenever I thought of hospitals, I thought of sick people and death. Old, sick people go to hospitals and then they die. My mind starting racing: Was my Mom going to die? It never occurred to me that she could die; just not be there in the morning when I woke or not be waiting for me in our maroon Oldsmobile Super 88 when school let out in the afternoon. At some subconscious level, however, I must have recognized the possibility of her death that cold winter day in 1968, because I set out to bargain with God. I marched into my bedroom and knelt before the silver and mother-of-pearl crucifix hanging above my bed. I prayed and bargained. "Please, God. Don't let her die. You can fix it so that I won't graduate from the 6th grade." In my mind, it was a good bargain, since failure to graduate was the ultimate disgrace. Only reprobates and delinquents didn't move up to the next grade. Louie had failed a grade in elementary school and one in junior high and was held back twice. It was a stigma. So, here was my bargaining chit. I say under by breath as I stare at the little dead body hanging on the cross, "Please, God, don't take mommy from me. I'll do anything."

The first night my Mom was in the hospital after her operation, Uncle Bruno and Auntie Mary and their son Little Johnny came to Torrington to visit her. Only my uncle said that he would stay home with "Tosca's kids," as he called us. My brothers and I weren't allowed to go visit my Mom that night, because she was too sick, we were told. I don't think my Mom wanted us to see her, weak and debilitated, in a hospital bed. Somehow, she knew the very thought of this would be too horrifying for Ricci and me. And, it would have been. So, my Dad, Nonni Upstairs and Auntie Mary went to Charlotte Hungerford Hospital to visit her. And something strange and incomprehensible happened to me that night.

Ricci and I were sitting at the kitchen table doing our homework, and my uncle came up behind my chair and grabbed my *petti*. I kept trying to push him away, and he finally left me alone. I didn't understand what was happening. Ricci was sitting there the entire time, so apparently my Uncle didn't do anything he was embarrassed about. So, why did I feel that there was something wrong with this? What had I done for him to do such a thing to me? I felt very ashamed. Something must be wrong with me, I thought. And somehow I knew I couldn't tell anyone; after all, my Uncle was highly respected by all the Riccucci's; his air of formality and gravity put him beyond reproach. Thereafter, every time I saw Uncle Bruno, I avoided him like the plague.

After my mother's operation the first week in March, my father and Nonni Upstairs took Ricci, me and Johnny to visit her in Charlotte Hungerford Hospital, the only hospital in Torrington. It was located on top of a big, lonely steep hill. It was foreboding; it looked like an eerie, dark, oppressive haunted house, and it gave me the shivers whenever we drove passed it. Walking into the vestibule of the hospital was like walking into a dimly lit, sinister, menacing alley. A giant, ominous oil painting of the hospital's benefactress Charlotte Hungerford hung on one of the walls; the drab green, brown and yellow oils made her look like an ogre. Walking through the narrow halls was no better. It smelled funny, too; like mothballs, cat pee, and old people's crotch. We had to talk softly and running or laughing was forbidden, my grandmother warned. Believe me, it was the last thing I thought of doing.

I was afraid to see what my Mom would look like; I started shaking. "Daddy, would you carry me?" I asked. "Sure *bambola*," or doll, which he always called me, and he swept me up into his arms. I was an anomalously tall, lanky eleven-year-old, standing in my bare feet at 5'5" weighing only 100 pounds. My grandmother yelled at me for being such a baby saying I was too old to be carried; "*che vergogna*," (how shameful) she kept whispering under her breath as we walked through the halls. I ignored her. I wrapped my skinny arms and legs around my father so tightly, he could barely walk. His familiar smell of Old Spice was now attenuated by a musty sweat. My Dad must have been scared, too, because he held me back just as tight.

As we rounded the corner of the hallway to her room, the sight of sick people sitting or walking in the hallway made me shudder; one guy was walking around with a ratty bathrobe and paper slippers, pulling a tall metal pole with a bag of pee hanging from one of the hooks. I had no idea what that was but it made me shut my eyes tightly and clutch my father's neck more intensely.

When we reached my mother's room, my Dad put me down and I stood frozen for a moment in that spot. As we started toward the drawn curtain, I grabbed his hand tightly and began shaking again. My mother was lying in a twin-sized bed with metal railings pulled up along the sides; she was tightly tucked into all-white bed linens. She tilted her head slowly in our direction as we walked in, and a small smile slowly stretched across her ashened face. I forgot how scared I was and ran over to the bed, bowed my long body over the bed rail and wrapped my arms around her. I started to cry. She comforted me, saying "don't cry Norminia, I'm o.k." I said "I miss you, Mommy and want you to come home; Bebe (our dog) misses you, too." She smiled at me, wiping away my tears with her thin, weak hands. If she had the strength, I wouldn't even have resisted a habit of hers that normally sent me squirming: her dabbing a tissue with spittle and wiping my dirty face. I continued to press my face into the side of her face and even though it smelled like a mixture of witch hazel and alcohol, it felt so soft and safe. I could have stayed like that forever. But, Nonni Upstairs came over, lowered the bed rail and gently pulled me away, saying I shouldn't worry my mother, because she was too weak. Half ignoring her, I scooted down to the bottom of the bed and wrapped my skinny little arms around her legs, and listened as my father and grandmother asked how she was feeling and how long before she would be coming home.

We were only allowed to stay for about fifteen minutes, the testy, unattractive nurse with the big boobs commanded, so as not to tire my mom. I didn't want to leave my Mom, but another side of me wanted to leave this awful hospital. I hugged her head, looked into her eyes, now just thin slits trying to stay open and, as I kissed her goodbye asked, "When are you coming home, Mommy." She whispered, "Very soon, honey." As we walked out of the room, I turned to wave, but her weary eyes were closed.

As we walked back through the hospital, I kept seeing the vision of my mother weak and frail in the hospital bed; it made me cry. By the time we got home, I had the worst case of diarrhea I could ever recall. I wished Mom was home to help me feel better, as she always did.

When she returned home, my Mom stayed in bed a lot. She still worked with Nonni Upstairs to prepare dinner, and she sat at the table with us, but she barely ate anything. She wore her powder-blue, quilted bathrobe and was stockingless in her black cotton slippers. I don't recall ever seeing her without a dress and nylon stockings with the reinforced toe. Her face looked pasty white, and she couldn't move around a lot. Her elbow rested on the dinner table, her hand propping up her head as she rearranged the food on her plate. She had pillow hair.

After dinner, she rarely sat with the family to watch television, a nightly ritual that was more about bonding than watching some of the funny shows on T.V., like "Bewitched," "The Andy Griffith Show," and "Hazel." Our black and white G.E. received reception, snowy at best, for only one station—CBS. Johnny usually lay on the floor in front of the T.V., while Ricci and I would pick a parent to sit with. We either crowded my mother on the red leather-upholstered rocking chair, or curled up with my father on the living-room sofa. We never asked; we just plopped down with one. It never occurred to us that they would be uncomfortable or just wanted some space to themselves. They would smile and enfold us in the safety of their arms.

My Mom was just too frail and weak now to sit up and watch T.V. with us. She stayed in bed. I didn't much like this, so I often crawled into bed with her in the early evenings. She would be groggy, probably from the pain medicine. And her skin was as papery as onion peel. But she gave me her attention, as I lay there chattering away about school, my friends or whatever popped into my head. She'd smile or softly ask questions.

And did I love to talk. On every report card I brought home from grammar school, there was always some remark written rather politely in the comment section about my loquaciousness: "Talks too much during class;" "A chatterbox;" "Distracts other students due to her chatty nature;" "Had to move Norma's seat several times for talking too much." I blamed it on the mind-numbing, unengaging lessons and teachings on the three R's— writing, reading and arithmetic—we trudged through every day. The most important thing I remember having learned in grammar school was to "duck and cover."

Lying in bed next to her, I went on and on about how I got in trouble that day in school for talking too much. I was always turning every which way in my desk to talk to classmates in the front, back or sides of me. I told my Mom how Mr. Tokarz, my 6th grade teacher, walked up to me, grabbed the crown of my head, and physically turned me around in my seat to face the front of the classroom. He later, also for talking, took me out of the lunch line and put me in the "dunce" line, as I called it. Standing off to the side, we were forced to eat our lunch after everyone else had finished, and even worse, we didn't get seconds. This was particularly upsetting on this day, because it was tuna salad on an English muffin day, with a brownie for dessert. And that delicious chunky potato salad would be scooped onto our plates by the cafeteria ladies with the lunchroom arms— that beefy, flab of flesh that hung down and shook when they served you. Tuna on a muffin was one of my favorites, because we never ate such American delicacies in my home. To the extent we ate "sangwitches," they consisted of green and red peppers fried up in olive oil with a few slices of provolone cheese on American bread. Or, *cicoria*, dandelion greens, fried in lots of oil and garlic with sweet sausage on a homemade *panino*. (I always scrapped off the *cicoria*, not because I didn't like the taste, but because my grandmothers picked the greens from our front and back yards; the thought of a dog freely pissing or crapping on them utterly repulsed me.) Or, the rustic sangwitch: a thick slice of homemade Italian bread, covered with very green olive oil, and a light coating of the meat of a garden-fresh, crimson-ripened tomato, smushed all over the surface.

I was really upset that day, I told my mother, for having to stand in the dunce line, eat last, and not get seconds; not to mention Joe, the school janitor, who got me a few times with his thick yardstick. Joe was a corpulent, dark Italian guy who would walk slowly through the lunch lines, a bit hunched over, and wack anyone who was talking too much. Everyone laughed at those who were cracked on the legs with his stick; but it wasn't very funny when you yourself were the object of his attention. This was an era when parents believed in corporal punishment as a way to make kids toe the line. So, as I expected, my

Mom didn't show me any sympathy when I told her about Joe's yardstick cracking across my right calf.

I also went on about how Mr. Tokarz made everyone in that dunce line, count the head hairs on the person in front of him or her. And, like an idiot, I did so only to keep my mind off my disgruntled belly.

My mother was lying on her side and she was facing me, her hair matted down from being on the pillow most of the day. She continued to gaze at me with her sleepy eyes, blinking her lids slowly and heavily, as I chattered away, legs crossed, with one swinging and bouncing away. She had a quiet sadness in her eyes. Never once did she say, *basta*, enough, keep quiet.

My Mom was never told she had cancer. Only my father knew. When she was diagnosed in February, my father was told she had six months to live. In those days, the person with the fatal disease was never told. I'm not really sure why; maybe it had something to do with a general belief that people fear death. So why tell someone they're going to die, whipping them into a state of frenzy or apoplexy, when there was nothing that could be done about it anyway? Within two-and-a half months, my mother's insides had rotted out and she was dead.

My Dad was alone with the knowledge that my Mom had the dreaded C-word; that ugly word conjured up fear and panic for me; it almost always spelled death back then so I'm glad Dad never told any of us. In retrospect, my Dad's own demise seemed to coincide with my mother's sealed fate. I'm not sure anyone really understood how very dependent my father was on my mother or how panicked he was with the prospect of losing her. One sign of his fear, although it didn't fully register with me at the time, was how he started acting really weird after we learned my Mom was sick; like the time he went out and bought an inordinate supply of canned sweet pink Del Monte grapefruit juice after my mother had expressed a strong liking for it. Anytime I went looking for my favorite cookies, Hydrox and Cameo, all I found were these large 24 oz. cans of that juice. They completely filled our upstairs' cupboards and took up most of our dry-food pantry in the basement. There were about a half a dozen cans chilling in the upstairs refrigerator, and about a dozen in the downstairs refrigerator. My Dad must have thought that somehow, if the supply of juice was endless, my mother would live to drink it.

It was also strange that my Dad, who never wanted any of us to travel very far from home, bought all of us, including Nonni Upstairs, plane tickets to Italy. My mother, ever since she had first stepped foot on Italian soil when she was only eight years old, longed to return to her native country. My Dad came home from work one night with 5 Pan Am tickets to Italy and several red-and-black plaid cloth suitcases. He said with a big smile on his face, "I got them at cost from Sears Roebuck." My eyes lit up when I saw those little suitcases; I yelled, "This one's mine," and promptly grabbed one, ran to my bedroom and gently slid it under the bed; this, I thought would be a nice replacement for the hatbox which held all of my charms, trinkets, gumball toys, matchbox cars, small weathered baseball glove, and my bendable Gumby and Pokey. My father must have purchased the tickets to instill hope in my Mom for her recovery. We were all excited about the prospect of going to Italy, especially me, because everyone in my family spoke so lovingly of it, even those, such as my Dad, who had never been there. Mom would not live to take this trip.

I didn't hear the phone ring. The hospital called my Dad sometime after midnight on May 22nd. Mom had returned to the hospital four days before, for a "check-up" my brothers and I were told. By the time my father arrived at the hospital, my mother was already in a pre-death coma state. She died shortly afterwards. My Dad, in complete despair, drove to Avon, Connecticut to the home of our good friends, Lucia and Compare. Lucia and Giuseppe, who we called Compare, or godfather, were very close friends of my maternal grandparents and of my parents. Compare immigrated to America around the same time as my grandparents and settled in Hartford where they met and became lifelong friends. Ever since I can remember, Compare and Lucia owned and operated a pizza house, Rotondo's, in Avon, Connecticut. Sometimes we would stop in on our way home from a Sunday dinner at Aunt Mary and Uncle Bruno's, who lived just outside Hartford. They made the best pizza and they would let my brothers and I stand in the kitchen and watch as the pizzas were pounded and tossed, slathered with red sauce and mozzarella and then shoved in and out of those huge, industrial ovens. Compare was my mother's baptismal godfather and hence, the nickname. Because I was so tall and gangly, he called me *stecchino*, or toothpick. As I grew older and more sinewy and slender, he called me two-by-four. My mother in turn, was the Commare, or godmother to their first born, Dolores. Like her father, Dolores had a pet name for me: initially she called me *culo secco*, or dried out rump because I was so skinny. By the time I was five, she was calling me *caca doso* (shit in your pants) because once when my Mom took Dolores and my brothers and me to Barkhamsted Lake in Litchfield County, Ricci and I were competing to see who could burp or fart the loudest. When it was my turn to fart, without knowing or feeling it, a tiny *cachi* slipped out of my hatch and into the crotch of my bathing suit. Ricci laughed, but I cried because Johnny scared me, yelling real loud, "You're gonna get a lickin' now!" My Mom didn't even holler at me; she just pulled the car over into a wooded area, cleaned me up with napkins and put me in a spare bathing suit. When I was seven, Dolores called me "vomit," because when my parents took her and my brothers and me to New York City to see the Statue of Liberty and the Empire State Building, I was so car sick that my Dad had to pull the car over every twenty minutes for me to puke. As much as I disliked the moniker, I preferred it to *caca doso*.

Dolores would eventually be my brother Ricci's godmother. Old world Italians like my grandparents and parents found a way to intertwine their lives with *paesani* in an effort to stay connected with their traditions and customs.

Lucia later told us, "I heard someone opening the kitchen door at about three o'clock in the morning" (no one locked their doors back then). My Dad didn't knock at the door; he just proceeded to walk softly up the stairs toward Lucia and Compare's bedroom. "I don't know why, but I sensed it was your father," she explained, and "I called out 'George?' Your Dad was crying and I knew that your mother must have died. I knew how sick she was. Then we drove to your house."

As Lucia recounted the story, I thought, "Why did Daddy go to Lucia instead of to Nonno who lived next door or to my Uncle Freddy and Auntie Gloria, who lived in the two-family house next to ours?" I wouldn't find out until a few years later.

I awoke in the early morning to the soft, muted cries of my father. The sounds were coming through the walls from my parent's bedroom, just next to mine. I could hear my brother Johnny consoling him: "It'll be okay, Daddy." I felt a sudden wave of panic, jumped out of bed and ran to my Dad. Johnny was in his pajamas, holding my father, who was sitting on the edge of his unmade, disheveled, bed, sobbing. His head was resting on Johnny's shoulder. Aside from my mother, Johnny, who was only 15 at the time, was the strong one in the family. He rarely cried; he held his sadness inside. I asked in a panicky, trembling voice, "What's wrong?" My father, whose eyes were swollen red, looked up at me and weepingly said, "God took your mother." I ran crying to my Dad, burrowing my face in his neck, hoping to stop the fright that was slowly creeping through my body. I just kept clutching onto my father, unable to let him go. Through my hyperventilating, convulsive bawling I asked, "Daddy is it going to be okay?" And for some reason I asked, "I don't have to go to school today, do I?" Dad shook his head no.

Then, I heard this loud reverberating scream coming from upstairs. "*È morta?*" I will never forget the sorrowful, heart-wrenching cry of Nonni Upstairs when Lucia told her that her *floria* Tosca, her beloved daughter was dead. My mother was sick, but the thought of her dying must have never entered Nonni's mind. It sounded operatic, like the lugubrious cries of Tosca when she learned that her lover Mario Cavaradossi was dead. Tosca was betrayed into believing that his death would be staged; a mock execution. But he was dead, and Tosca screams out "*Morto? Tu? Così? Finire così?*" (You? Dead like this? Is this how it ends?) just before she throws herself off the parapet of the castle, *Castel Sant'Angelo*.

That sound, those words, "*È morta?*" both frightened me and saddened me, because of the inner hollowness they conveyed. They will ring forever in my head. My mother was dead and I would never, ever see her again, touch her again, hold her again, or feel safe by her embrace again. I am very angry. I had prayed hard, but God didn't meet his end of the bargain. I felt betrayed—by God and by death.

The day was numbing. Word of my Mom's death must have spread quickly throughout the neighborhood, because people kept coming to the house throughout the day, dropping off food. It reminded me of when Nonni Next Door died three years earlier. That was my first encounter with death, and it was exceedingly confusing to me—there was a pall of incredible sadness, yet there was also a celebration. Everyone in the neighborhood, including the Favali's, Mastro's, Marciano's, Vedivelli's, Avenia's and countless others, stopped by at different points during the day with bowls of pasta, green salads, soups, breads, cookies, pies and cakes. Food was their expression of sorrow for the death of my grandmother. I don't remember much of that day, except my Mom consoling my Dad, and Johnny following Ricci and me around, trying to distract us from the gloom and anguish which permeated our house that day. He would occasionally interject some levity about the food being brought into the house, not commenting on who brought the food, just something about the food. When Mrs. Leonard brought in a blueberry pie, Johnny commented, "Wow, look at that big ole pie. I'm going to put my whole face in that pie and slurp it all up." It seemed to work because Ricci and I would look at each other, almost for permission from one another to smile or giggle; and we did. Johnny could be such an annoying sycophant most of the time, but I was grateful that day for his tender loving care.

But, this after-death party was now for Mom, and I didn't want any part of it. I tried to stick by my Auntie Gloria, who was busy trying to organize the onslaught of food and dealing with all the neighbors. I followed her around for a short time, wrapping my arms around her waist, her hugging me back real tight. But, I didn't want the neighbors to see me vulnerable and crying. At least I could count on Ricci. We barely said a word to each other. We just wandered around together, from room to room, back and forth, from our house to Nonno's to Uncle Freddy and Auntie Gloria's.

Periodic wailing from Nonni Upstairs pierced my skull. She would scream something out in Italian—*Dio, come la potrebbe fa questo?* (God, how could you do this?) or *Non ci Dio più per me ora* (There is no God for me now). Johnny, with stoic practicality, was glued to her side all day; it seemed to provide her with some solace. Just as when Nonni Next Door died, Johnny never shed a tear. That always baffled me. "Why didn't he cry for Mommy?" I thought. Ricci and I were afraid to go near Nonni. Every time she screamed out her pain, Ricci and I fled. At one point we ran into my parent's bedroom and closed the door. My Dad's bed was still unmade and we lay down on the crumpled up sheets. We just laid there staring up at the ceiling, occasionally glancing at one another for reassurance and comfort.

At one point I asked Ricci, "Where's Daddy?" He said, "Uncle Livio and Uncle Freddy are taking care of him." I guessed that he must have needed to be with his brothers. I felt selfish because I kept thinking, "I wish Daddy was here with me and Ricci." Even with Ricci by my side, I felt alone. I began to feel anger welling up inside of me. I was angry with God, who didn't fulfill our bargain. I told Ricci, "I'll be right back," and jumped off the bed and marched into my bedroom, closing the door behind me. I walked over to my bed, took my shoes off—Mommy didn't allow me on the bed with my shoes—jumped up on my pillows, leaned against the headboard, and made eye contact with Jesus, whose eyes were barely open, him hanging on the crucifix half dead and all. I was just about to bawl him out for not keeping what I thought was a deal, his promise to me, when the door to my room opened, startling me. It was my cousin Audrey.

I think Audrey thought I was praying, rather than reaming Jesus out, because she silently sat down on the edge of my bed and assumed the prayer-like position: clasped hands, lowered head, eyes closed. I didn't say anything to her; I just cried.

I was heartbroken; not because I fully understood at eleven what my mother's absence from my life would feel like for the remainder of my life on earth; but because she was gone, and I never got to say goodbye to her.

I didn't know it at the time, but this singular event, my mother's death, would prove to be the most profound, fateful experience in my life, not only because of the void it would create and forever be felt—no matter how old we grow to be, we'll always yearn for the primordial safety, love and affection of our mothers—but also because her death would set off a series of seemingly unending events that would haunt me and my brothers for the rest of our lives.

How could God do this? She was only 46 years old, which maybe wasn't so old after all. How could he betray my mother, who was the kindest, gentlest soul? She never hurt anyone and was loved by everyone. She truly was the eponymous *Tosca*:

> *Vissi d'arte, vissi d'amore, non feci mai*
> *male ad anima viva . . . .*
> *Nel'or dell delore*
> *perchè Signore,*
> *perchè me ne rimuneri così?*

> I lived for art and love; and I never
> harmed a soul . . . .
> Now, in my hour of need,
> Why God?
> Why have you repaid me in this way?

Act II. Scene 4. Tu Più Non Torni

(*"You will Never Return,"* from
Puccini's *La Bohème*)

For what seemed like the longest time, all of us—me, my father, brothers, and grandparents—just stood there in front of the casket with my mother's lifeless body, holding each other, crying.

I remember moving closer to her, peering down at her hands, folded neatly across her chest. "What an odd thing to do with her hands," I thought. I placed my hand on top of hers, and it felt stiff and cold as glass.

I pulled my hand away very abruptly and asked, "Daddy, why is her hand so cold?" He just continued to cry.

I was looking intently at her pallid, still face and was again struck by fear when I spotted a very thin, black jagged line between her lips and between her closed eyes, where the upper and lower eyelids met. I blurted out "Daddy, why does it look like she has stitches in her lips and eyes?"

He lied through his tears, "Don't worry honey, it's just the make-up they use." Then we sat down. But, it didn't look like eyeliner, mascara or lip liner to me.

My father, brothers and I sat up front in the funeral parlor just off to the side of my mother's casket. People streamed in all evening. I didn't even know who some of these people were. It made me realize how many friends my mother had; how much she was loved by others, and how many lives she had touched. I kept looking over at Mom, somehow expecting her to wake up and climb out of the casket. A few times, I think I saw her move.

At the end of the evening, when no one but the immediate family was in the room, we again stood by the casket. I reached out to Mom's hand again; it was still cold, but this time I kept my hand on hers. Then, without any forethought, I stood on my tippy toes, hunched my body over the casket and kissed her on the lips, my tears streaming down, streaking her made-up face. It felt as though I was kissing a plastic doll, and that blackness in-between her lips and eyes still confused and scared me. I gently stroked her face, closed my eyes and then softly pressed my cheek up against hers, now cold and lifeless, and stayed like that until someone—probably Nonni Upstairs—pulled me away. I wondered, "Did they forget to put her nylon stockings with the reinforced toe and favorite high-heels on, the ones that matched her dress and hat?"

We were told it was time to go. I asked my father if I could see her entire body, not just the top half. Auntie Mary, who overheard my request, asked why. I said, "I just want to see all of her." I guess I wanted to make sure she was all there. What if she was sawed in half? My father didn't even question my request, and walked up to Mr. LaPorta and asked "Can the bottom half of the casket be opened for my little girl?" When my father returned, he said, it couldn't be opened. I protested but to no avail. It made me suspicious as to whether they really did dress her in nylon stockings and her favorite, matching high-heel shoes.

It was hard to leave the room and my mother's body. My father had to be escorted out by two men from the funeral home, because he didn't want to leave. My Dad was crying and pleading with Mr. Laporta "Please let me stay longer." I wondered, "How will my father survive this?" This image of my father struggling to remain with my mother even in death crushed me; it will forever remind me of *Tosca's* handsome Mario Cavaradossi, who laments his love for and impending loss of his beloved Tosca. I could almost hear the incipit of the melody, where the soft, hauntingly lonely notes of the clarinet pour out a wretched pain of loss. Cavaradossi sings:

> *E lucevan le stelle,*
> *ed olezzava la terra*
> *stridea l'uscio dell'orto*
> *e un passo sfiorava la rena.*
> *Entrava ella fragrante,*
> *mi cadea fra la braccia.*
> *O dolci baci, o languide carezze,*
> *mentr'io fremente le belle forme disciogliea dai veli!*
> *Svanì per sempre il sogno mio d'amore.*
> *L'ora è fuggita, e muoio disperato!*
> *E muoio disperato,*
> *e non ho amato mai tanto la vita!*

And the stars were shining,
and the earth smelled sweet,
the garden gate squeaked,
and a step brushed the sand.
She came in, fragrant,
and fell into my arms.
Oh sweet kisses, oh languid caresses,
while I, trembling, released her lovely features from
their veils!
Gone forever are my dreams of love.
The hour has fled, and I die in despair!
And I die in despair.
And with her, I have never loved life so much!

I was once again standing in the vestibule with my family,
and the door behind us, where my Mom laid, closed for
good. I am so glad I kissed her.

Dad ordered a fleet of black limousines for the funeral.

I sat in the back seat of the limo that was following the big black hearse, which had a small rear window, with petite, bright white laced curtains that were closed to hide the coffin. I sat very close to Ricci, the both of us staring out the window. We were catatonic, in a state of shock, but we were much too young to know, to fully comprehend the meaning of death, even though Nonni Next Door had died three years earlier.

The limos proceeded slowly from our house, down Main Street through the small town of Torrington. I glanced over at all the familiar places we passed along the way: the A&P where my Mom used to buy groceries, Jimmy's General Store, where every Sunday after church, my Dad took my brothers and me to buy a dime's worth of penny candy: tootsie rolls, squirrel nut zippers, caramel chews, BB Bats, Atomic Fireballs, Mary Janes, Bit-O-Honeys and Bazooka bubble gum. And Bob Crane's Esso gas station, where Ricci, Louie, Jimmy, Robbie and me rode our bikes to almost every day of every summer. Bob was the candy-corn lady's son; he always gave us free "STP" stickers for our bikes. Louie said "STP" stood for "Stop Teenage Pregnancy" or alternatively, "Scratchy Toilet Paper." The other reason we loved Bob's gas station was the soda machine. It was always well stocked with 6 oz. bottles of our favorite sodas, the kind we never got at home. It had Wink, Fresca, Sarsparilla, Birch Beer, Root Beer, Grape and Orange Nehi and, of course, Coca Cola. A bottle cost a quarter. At home, when we were allowed soda, it was ginger ale, what I called "old people's soda." I loved opening that long, skinny window on the soda machine to find the broad array of soda bottles stacked one on top of the other, identifiable only by the shinny bottle caps. I liked Wink, Birch Beer and Orange Nehi the best.

The procession ended at St. Peter's Church. We were ushered out of the car by some men in black suits, and lined up behind the casket. We slowly walked into the church, which was full of yet more family, friends, acquaintances, and neighbors. The sight of so many people made me cry.

I couldn't even laugh at the women with Kleenexes on their heads. Just before my Mom got sick, we were in church one Sunday morning, sitting in the pew waiting for mass to start and a smartly dressed woman sat down in the pew in front of us. She was wearing a Kleenex on her head, with two brown bobby pins holding down each side. In the 1960s, it was forbidden for a woman to enter the house of God without having her head covered. I never understood the rule, and once asked my Dad, "why do Mommy and I have to wear a hat and Ricci, Johnny and you don't?" He explained that it was impolite to God for a woman to expose her head in church, but also impolite if a man wore a hat. I thought it was a stupid rule. Ricci and I pointed our index fingers at the Kleenex-head and started snickering under our breaths. Johnny whispered, "What are you two laughing at?" My Mom kept shushing us: "Quiet you two; no laughing in church." Johnny would smirk at us for getting hollered at. But Ricci and I could hardly contain our giggles. Only it wasn't very funny the following Sunday, when I realized I had forgotten my white veil, the one I insisted on wearing instead of a hat. My Mom made me put a Kleenex on my head, magically pulling a bobby pin out of her virtually empty purse to secure it. I sulked and pouted pleading with my mother, "Mommy, please don't make me wear this." She shook her head and ignored me. During the mass, Ricci periodically pointed to my head and giggled. I scowled and gave him a good, hard elbow to his side, which abruptly stopped his snickering.

When we reached our pews, I looked up at the altar, where the flower-covered coffin had been placed on trestles. Dad was kneeling with his head buried in his arms, tears dropping to the empty space below him. I clutched his arm, and whispered in his ear, "Will we be able to see Mommy again?"

He whispered through his tears, "The casket can't be opened again," which made me want to run up to it, bang on it and pry it open.

"*Maybe she isn't even in there,*" I thought.

As I stared at the casket, I wondered, did Mommy know she was going to die? Did she wonder what would become of us? Did she want to leave us? The lyrics of *Senza Mama* played over and over in my head:

> *Ora che sei un angelo del cielo . . . .*
> *Tu puoi scendere giù pel firmamente ed aleggiare intorno a me,*
> *ti sento, sei qui, mi baci, m'accarezzi.*
> *Ah, dimmi quando in cielo potrò vederti? Quando potrò baciarti?*
> *Oh, dolce fine di ogni mio dolore!*
> *Quando in cielo con te potrò salire?*

Now that you are an angel in heaven . . .
You can come down from the sky and I feel you fluttering about me,
I feel you, you are here, you kiss me, caress me.

Oh, tell me when shall I see you in heaven? When shall I kiss you?
Oh, sweet end to all my sorrows!
When can I join you in Heaven?

I bawled my fists up so tight that my fingernails started cutting into the palms of my hands. I was still pissed at Jesus for taking my Mom, so when it was time to receive Holy Communion, I whispered to Dad, "I don't want communion." He said, "You have to!"

I attempted to rationalize, "But I haven't been to confession."

He quietly responded, "Just say an Act of Contrition."

Before receiving the Eucharist, Catholics are required to confess their sins to a priest sitting in a confessional booth, which resembles a large armoire with a door in the middle—where the priest gets in—and two compartments on each side. At Saint Peter's, thick, blood-red velvet curtains covered the front of each compartment so as to hide the confessor. Once in the compartment, the confessor kneels on a narrow wooden kneeler and waits for the priest to slide open a widow in the middle of the compartment panel. A thin latticed metal screen separates the priest from the penitent. When the window opens, the confessor makes the sign of the cross and rotely declares, "Bless me father for I have sinned, my last confession was (fill in the blank)."

Only mortal sins—breaking one of the Ten Commandments—need to be confessed to God via the priest; venial sins were forgiven without the middleman by simply reciting the Act of Contrition. Only then could one take communion, the holy, tasteless wafer which incarnated the body of Christ. I never understood why we ate Christ, thought it was cannibalistic, but went along with it because if I didn't, I'd burn in hell. Father Sal instructed us to never, ever let the host touch our teeth, because this would be disrespectful to Jesus and desecrate his holy name. Only the tongue and the roof of the mouth could have contact with the body of Christ.

I took communion at St. Peter's that day, but furtively ground the host between by teeth.

After the mass, we piled into the limos again, and were driven off to St. Francis's cemetery. The cemetery was like a small little town, with narrow little roads, and virtually no traffic. I was very familiar with it because I had been here many times with my father, who for the last three years, had come every morning to visit Nonni Next Door's grave. Ricci and I looked forward to going with him on Saturdays and Sundays because my Dad let us drive in the cemetery. By the time I turned seven, I was learning how to drive. I would sit next to my Dad in his truck and he'd let me steer the wheel and shift the gears. The truck was a three-on-the column and when it was time to shift my father would call out, "shift." I'd say, "Daddy, I know when to shift; you don't have to tell me every time, because I can see when you punch in the clutch that it's time to shift. Promise you won't say it again, okay?"

"Okay," he'd say but continued to call out "shift" when it was time. Within a few years, I was able to sit behind the wheel and drive on my own, on condition my Dad was with me.

Nonni Next Door had a huge tombstone, with a very large plot; it was big enough for her husband, three sons, and their wives. Daddy tended to the flowers at her grave, while Ricci and I went to the closest faucet and filled a pail with water. We then knelt and prayed silently. If Ricci had driven to the gravesite, I drove out toward the exit. I always took the long way around, by the *Pietá* tombstone that was the grandest in the whole of the cemetery.

Driving to the cemetery now somehow felt very, very different. Neither Ricci nor I would ever ask Dad again to let us drive through this despairing little town.

ACT III. SCENE 1.
SENZA MAMMA

("*With no Mother*," from Puccini's *Suor Angelica*)

A month after my Mother died, I got my first period.

I was outside playing, and felt a little creepy between my legs. I went to the bathroom and there it was; the bloods. I pulled up my pants and went crying to my grandmother, who made a face, waved a hand at me and said in Italian, "you better get used to it; it's a woman's lot." She gave me some enormous pads to wear that were the size of the red bricks Uncle Livio used to build houses. Apparently, they were some sort of hospital pads that my mother used after her operation, and there was a mountainous leftover supply in Mom's closet. My ever frugal grandmother had saved them and now thought I might as well use them. "Why do I have to wear these big, fat pads?" I complained to my grandmother. But she simply said in her matter-of-fact manner, "You're lucky; in our days we had to use rags, which we had to wash out every night." Yuck, I thought to myself. Until that supply of pads was gone, for five days out of every month, I walked around bowl-legged, cowboy style, with a mammoth, padded clump—safety pinned to my underwear—between my legs. The boys, especially Louie, teased me unmercifully. "Hey Norma; you on the rag?" "Shut your clam hole, you big stupid pig," I would yell back. I now realized where that awful phrase "she's on the rag" came from. To avoid embarrassment, I just stayed indoors until my period stopped. I wished Mom was here.

Nonni Upstairs was from the old school and insisted I wear ridiculously outdated dresses that she bought at Sears Roebuck. "Nonni, I'm not wearing these clothes to school. Everyone will laugh at me!" She bellowed, "Why do you always give me a hard time. Your brothers never talk back to me. You are a Riccucci through and through." I shot back, "And proud of it!" At which point she grabbed a handful of my hair and yanked it.

I felt an overwhelming sense of shame every day I went to school. Plus, I was just not pretty. I was tall, too, but I never minded this before. But now I was in seventh grade at Vogel Junior High where students came from everywhere in Torrington; aside from Catholic parochial schools, it was the only junior high in town. The kids from elementary school knew not to mess with me, but now I was among strange, unfamiliar faces.

To make matters worse, Nonni wouldn't allow me to shave my legs. Italian women do not shave; anywhere! And our hair is thick and dark. I really must have looked like a refugee to my classmates. A sartorial burp. "Hey, you're gonna need a sickle or a bushwhacker to cut that thick forest," the girls hissed. In a typical, juvenile tit-for-tat kind of way, I'd yell back, "Why don't you do us all a favor and go play in heavy traffic." They persisted. "Gorilla legs!"

I shut them up, even shocked them when I yelled, "Fuck off."

I thought to myself, "No wonder why my grandmothers swore so much; it is extraordinarily powerful." It was at this point that I learned the power of expletives. And "fuck" was a powerful word. It sounded better, harsher in English, though. All the swear words I learned in Italian from my grandmothers were too pretty—*catsone*, *stronso*, *cagna*, *vaffanculo*—and just not as coarse or cathartic as shithead, asshole, bitch, fuck you. Girls weren't supposed to use such foul language, so it made it all the more jarring. It was the next best thing to flinging someone. It was Nonni Upstairs who taught me to take only so much crap from anyone. One of her trademark sayings came to be: "*si può spingere un ombrello su il mi culo, ma non l'apre* (you can shove an umbrella up my ass, but just don't open it). It sounds more flowery in Italian, but the graphic illustration is quite pointed (no pun intended).

But it was all very humiliating and gave me a complex about wearing skirts or dresses. And, of course, Nonni Upstairs wouldn't allow me to wear pants to school. She gave an emphatic "no" to wearing overalls, as she called them, which, in her broken English, sounded like "rubber hose." She rhetorically asked, "Why can't you be how your mother was, and dress more elegantly?" "Why can't you be like mommy, and let me wear what I want!" I shot back, then ran to avoid *uno schiaffo in testa* (a smack in the head).

"Poor, Nonni," I thought. "Why do I give her such a hard time?" She's got to be in great pain from losing her daughter. She loves me very much, I know, but does she have to be so harsh and critical, not to mention practical and bossy? I just wished she could be more affectionate like Mom. No matter, I kept wearing my dungarees after school and on weekends, and I vowed to myself that when I was old enough to make decisions about my own wardrobe, I would never, ever wear a skirt or dress again. God, I'm like a freak.

I implored my Dad to intervene. "Daddy, please tell Nonni to let me shave my legs or at least wear pants to school." But Dad was no longer present. Without Mom around, he was an empty shell. His entire body had sunk, and his skin always had a chalky, nervous sweaty look to it. He was completely unanimated, and he never said a word unless you asked him a question. "*Bambola*, you have to do what your grandmother tells you because your mother is not here," he said. "But, Daddy, can't you just stand up to her for just this once?" I whined. He sighed, shook his head and walked away. I felt anger toward him, which brought out the guilt in me. Mom's death broke his heart, so I why am I being such a pain in the ass?

At some point, it became too stressful to ride the bus to school, so my Dad started driving Ricci and me to school in his pickup truck on his way to work in the morning. Ricci went along with this, to stick by me as he always did. Johnny, who went to Torrington High, continued to ride the bus. Given my father's work schedule, we got dropped off at least a half-hour before school started. But I didn't want to wait in front of the school for fear of more harassing, so Daddy dropped us off at the corner, about 1/6th of a mile away from school. There was a U.S. Post Office on the corner and Ricci and I would loaf around outside until we heard the first bell at Vogel. In the winter, we started going inside the post office to keep warm. We pretended to be busy writing out letters or studying the "wanted" posters hanging on the wall. A postal clerk was soon on to us and kicked us out, yelling, "You kids can't hang around, loitering in the post office; this is a federal building and private property." Normally, I would have challenged him, but in this case decided not to open my big mouth, since this man was obviously in a position of considerable authority; after all, he was wearing a postal uniform. The winter days seemed cold and long.

Just before I decided to stop riding the bus in the mornings, Ronnie Freedman and I got kicked off for an entire week. Ronnie was one of my buddies for a good part of my childhood. I was five years old when she and her parents moved into our neighborhood and we quickly became best friends. The Freedman's were Jewish, both my grandmothers found it necessary to point out to me. I wasn't sure what it meant to be Jewish, especially since Ronnie seemed like everyone else I knew. We were the same age and even started school together. In fact, except for some of the weird-tasting foods she used to give me, there didn't seem to be any differences between us at all. Yet, some of the neighborhood kids made a big deal of the fact that Ronnie was Jewish; I called them dumbbells and just ignored them.

Even after Ronnie had moved away from Greenridge Road, we remained close, at least until seventh grade when she joined the other classmates who made disparaging remarks about my clothes, hairstyle, or hairy legs. I don't think she really wanted to participate in the heckling, but would herself have become the object of the derision if she didn't. Most everyone succumbs to peer pressure, because no one wants to be an outsider.

This one afternoon, Ronnie and I were riding home on the bus together. She sat alongside me and started needling me about my matted-down leg hair protruding through my pantyhose. She asked, "Why don't you at least wear darker stockings, Norma, so all that hair won't stick out?" I looked out the window and ignored her. She then started complaining about the female bus driver's rule that boys sit in the front of the bus, girls in the back. On one level, we recognized that separating the sexes no doubt made it easier for the bus driver to keep everyone in line, but on another, we saw something inherently wrong with one, segregating the sexes, and two, making the girls invariably sit at the back of the bus.

So, Ronnie and I sauntered up to a seat in the front of the bus and completely ignored the bus driver's repeated requests for us to move to the back of the bus. The bus driver eventually pulled the bus over to the side of the road, turned to face us and yelled, "I'm giving youse one last chance to move to dah backa dah bus." We again continued our conversation and didn't even glance up at her.

The next day we were both summoned to the principal's office where Vice-Principal Andersen barred us from bus services for a full week. "Mrs. Kowalski said that you two girls were making trouble on the bus yesterday," he said. "You broke the rules so, now you'll have to find another way to get to school for one whole week." Ronnie just shrugged it off, but I panicked and my eyes welled up with tears. Nonni Upstairs would kill me over this one. What would I do? And, then, for some inexplicable reason, I blurted out, "My mother's dead; how will I get to school in the morning?" I couldn't stop the words from coming out of my mouth. I regretted the outburst, because Ronnie looked at me disapprovingly and said, "My Mom will pick you up."

So, for the next week, I got off to the bus stop in the morning at the regular time so as not to tip my grandmother off that something was wrong, and waited for Sally and Ronnie to pick me up. I never told my grandmother because she would have severely punished me. I did tell my father, who was too depressed to notice or care, and my brother Ricci, who roared with laughter about the incident and called me a reprobate.

There was something about this entire incident that made me not so much invincible, but rebellious. I became somewhat iconoclastic, openly disagreeing or arguing with my teachers, just for the sake of being a nuisance. I would walk into classes late and commit the ultimate no-no: snapping my gum and blowing bubbles in class. Sometimes I got detention—I would tell my grandmother I was saying after school to play basketball—other times I'd be forced to stick my gum on the end of my nose and sit through the entire class with the rubbery blob stiffening at the end my nose. I really had nothing to lose.

Nonni Upstairs cried a lot now that Mommy was gone. I thought older people died before younger ones. Through all her pain, my grandmother, who had always had a hand in raising my brothers and I, became our sole parent, because my father was no longer capable of making parental decisions. She mourned for a long time.

Once, we were in the basement with Martha and the Vandellas blasting on our red-and-white portable RCA record player with the built-in speaker. Our neighbor, Christine Mastro was Martha Reeves, and Ricci and I were the Vandellas; we were pantomiming "Heat Wave" with a soulful fervent, when my grandmother yelled down in Italian, "turn off that music. Don't you know you shouldn't be playing music, your mother dead and all only three months ago?" Ricci and I, eyes bulging out of their sockets, froze in our tracks. I sheepishly turned the music off, and Chris asked us how long we'd have to wait before we could listen to music again or watch T.V., which we hadn't seen in these last three weeks. We never thought to ask our grandmother these questions. We just did what she told us, and felt guilty if we secretly missed T.V., music or any other amusement or merriment that had come to an abrupt halt in our lives. It seemed so long ago. My grandmother was still wearing black dresses, thick black stockings and her scuffed-up black patten-leather pumps.

Despite her grieving, Nonni upstairs was still quick to speak her mind. In public, this was rather embarrassing at times.

Nonni Upstairs loved shoes. She was forever walking into department stores and asking the first identifiable salesperson, "*Hai le* SHOOZ-eh?" I would, of course, be mortified, because the bewildered clerk would have no idea what on earth my grandmother was saying. So I or one of my two brothers would have to intervene, in a somewhat diffident manner, "We're looking for shoes."

Then, to completely throw us over the edge, once she found a pair of shoes she liked, she would try to bargain the price down as if she were in an outdoor Italian market. The thing about my grandparents was that, even though their knowledge of the English language was limited, they knew American currency. Money was paramount to any immigrant so, shrewdness with cash, whether dollars or lire, was fundamental. Interestingly enough, on a rare occasion Nonni Upstairs was successful in getting the price knocked down by arguing that the merchandise was damaged or something of that sort—"dis-sah SHOOZ-eh, it-sah SCRA-cheh," she would argue. Needless to say, I would be hiding out at the other end of the shoe department, pretending to shop for shoes.

ACT III. SCENE 2.
O MIO BABBINO CARO

("*Oh My Dear Little Father*," from
Puccini's *Gianni Schicchi*)

I awoke to a sudden thud.

It came from my father's bedroom. I jumped out of bed and ran across the hall to find my Dad lying on the floor. He was on his back, groping up at the air, helplessly trying to get up. I asked, as I tried to lift him back into his bed, "Daddy, are you okay?" He mumbled something incomprehensible, and I asked, "What's wrong, Daddy?" His face looked distorted and confused. I stood there a minute, looking at this giant of a man sprawled out on the floor in his pajamas. I felt a sudden fear when I realized that I wasn't strong enough to help him back into his bed; it was like lifting dead weight and I just couldn't do it. I stood there looking around the room, as if some idea would come to me; something that might help me get him back into his bed. I thought, "Should I put a blanket over him and wait until morning for him to get up for work?"

I recalled the night before when Ricci, Johnny, Nonni Upstairs and I returned home from my cousin Claudia's wedding at the Hilton Hotel in Hartford. It was about five months after my Mom had died. Claudia is on my Mom's side of the family, Aunt Mary and Uncle Bruno's oldest child. She was gorgeous; she looked like Annette Funicello. Her betrothed, Danny, was exceedingly handsome, although a divorcee, as Nonni Upstairs constantly reminded everyone. I was so happy to be here because it was a temporary break from the dark cloud that hovered over our home. It was a big Italian wedding, with an endless amount of food, dancing and trays upon trays of Italian cookies.

Dad said he had to keep his shoe store open, and so he couldn't come with us. No one thought anything of it, as he never closed his shoe store on Saturdays. When we returned around midnight from the wedding, my Dad was asleep. Since I never went to bed without kissing him goodnight, I tip-toed into his room and kissed him goodnight. He didn't even stir; he was in an eerie, deadened sleep. I stared at him for a minute or two, listened to his heavy breathing, and then dragged my tired carcass to bed.

I quietly went up to my brothers' room and woke up Johnny. "Johnny, something's wrong with Daddy." He came downstairs with me and tried to help our father up, but could not. He told me, "go get Nonni." Nonni Upstairs came down, took one look at my Dad and went to the phone to call Uncle Freddy. He and my Auntie Gloria came to our house, saw my father's state and immediately called an ambulance. I don't remember how long it took for the two men, who were dressed completely in white—pants, shirts and jackets—to arrive at our house. I began crying when I saw my poor father looking so helpless, being carried out, strapped down on a gurney, still pulling at the air, trying to get someplace, anyplace, but unable to get there. Nonni Upstairs kept shushing me, because it wasn't proper to cry in front of strangers, she said. I tried to run over to him, but Nonni held me back.

The next day while Ricci and I were doing our homework at the dining room table, we overheard Uncle Freddy talking quietly to Nonni Upstairs; they were in the living room and clearly didn't want us to hear their conversation. Ricci whispered, "What are they saying?" I said, "I can't hear. I'm gonna find out." I tiptoed to the doorway of the living room still out of their view and heard Uncle Freddy saying something about an overdose of sleeping pills. I went back to doing my homework and lied to Ricci, "I can't hear what they're talking about." I was confused. I knew my father had difficulty sleeping after Mom died, so I thought he accidentally took too many pills. I thought, "Why were Nonni and Uncle Freddy being so secretive about it?" It was only after his second suicide attempt that I realized that these weren't accidents.

Dad was in the intensive care unit at the Charlotte Hungerford Hospital. So, here we were again, floating it seemed, down the halls of the creepy hospital. This time I clung to Ricci. My Dad was hooked up to all sorts of machines, needles, tubes and bottles, from what I could see. I could barely stand to look; I got so close to his face that the only thing I could see was the black pools of his deep, sorrowful eyes. His long black eyelashes were slightly moist from tears or maybe the drugs running through him. I hugged him; his face felt like sandpaper against my cheek. I asked, "When are you coming home, Daddy?" He smiled slightly and said in a whisper "I don't know, *bambola*."

He was in the intensive care unit for about three days, after which they transferred him to a regular room. We visited him every night. After another week, he was transferred to the psychiatric unit of the hospital. I didn't understand why they put him in this unit with what appeared to be crazy people. I told Nonni Upstairs, "Daddy doesn't belong here with all these loopy people talking to themselves and walking around with their shriveled up old butts peeking out of the backs of their gowns." She just shook her head; nobody listened to what I had to say. We continued to visit him every night, and every night, he seemed sadder and lonelier than the previous night.

Even when my Mom was alive, my father never disciplined or spanked us. It was my mother who yelled at us if we did something wrong and gave us the occasional light swat on the butt. We were forewarned about a prospective whack because Mom would ball up her fist and bite the knuckle of her forefinger, the body language of an Italian who is either VERY angry or about to have an apoplectic fit. In any event, one knew to stand clear.

After Mommy died, Nonni Upstairs took over as disciplinarian. She had to; my father was too withdrawn to even communicate much with us, and now he was in the hospital. As an old-world Italian, my grandmother was a bit more liberal than my Mom in dispensing the physical punishment. She could be pretty cunning about it, too. One afternoon, I was chasing Ricci and teasing him unmercifully about girls. "You like Teresa Fasachese, and I'm gonna tell her in school tomorrow." He ran crying to my grandmother, like a big crybaby, so I got real mad and told him I was going to fling him real good. Nonni Upstairs called out for me: "*Norma, viene qui!*" I knew that if I went to her, she'd give me a hard smack upside the head. In an effort to avoid the punitive encounter, I ran and hid behind the garage. I figured that by the end of the day, she'd forget about the whole thing.

Later that evening, Nonni and my brothers and I were watching "That Girl" on television. We had finished dinner and my grandmother showed no sign of being angry with me. Phew, I thought; I'm home free.

I was lying on the couch, Ricci was sitting in the red leather rocking chair, Johnny was lying on the floor, and Nonni was sitting in her usual armchair by the picture window. We were relaxing with our highballs. My grandmother often fixed us highballs (three parts Canada Dry, one part Four Roses Whiskey, lots of ice cubes and a colored-glass swizzle stick) in the early evenings. Ricci and I had trouble sleeping after my Mom died. A nice highball, Nonni would say, is what we needed. So, here we were: I was 11, Ricci 12 and Johnny 14, and we were sitting around watching T.V., sipping highballs.

Nonni got up from her chair and started walking toward the kitchen. She made a B-line for me on the couch, grabbed and clutched me by the hair and pulled so hard I fell onto the floor. I began crying and holding on to the top of my aching head, which I am sure must have had clumps of hair ripped out of it. Ricci started to laugh uncontrollably; Johnny smirked and giggled. Without uttering a single word or sound, my grandmother returned to her chair, neatly smoothed the black dress under her butt and plopped down. She didn't forget about the incident during the day after all. From then on, I knew that when Nonni summoned me for a scolding, I would immediately go to her in order to avoid any unnecessary, nasty surprises.

After my father returned home from the hospital, I became frightened of sleeping in my bedroom. I was so petrified about what had happened when my Dad took the sleeping pills that I didn't want to be the one to hear another thud during the night. I told Johnny that I was afraid to sleep in my room, and asked if we could switch bedrooms. He must have understood, as did Nonni Upstairs, because he agreed to the move; Nonni who would have normally vetoed any such move didn't say a word about it. So, I started sleeping upstairs, in the bed next to Ricci's. Somehow, though, it didn't feel much like old times, when Ricci and I giggled and whisperd to each other until Nonni would come in brandishing a hairbrush yelling at us. I'll never forgive myself for making this move, because even though my Dad never said anything about it, I felt guilty, as though I had broken the strong bond between us.

I was maturing, growing up as they say. I no longer wanted to be "daddy's little girl," and resented any coddling from him. I was a grown-up now. I was also becoming bratty and impudent, finding fault in my Dad for small things, such as his buying the wrong size sanitary napkins for me. I was too embarrassed to stand at a cash register and pay for such a humiliating necessity, so I had my forever unabashed father buy them. Once, because the store didn't have the small Kotex brand I used, he brought home extremely large, generic pads. I caustically yelled at him, "I don't want these stupid things; they're huge, and I can't walk with them stuck in my crotch." My father walked away crushed, saying nothing.

And, so, I started spending less time with my Dad. The guilt I would feel for abandoning him would come back to haunt me most of my life.

My Dad never closed his shoe store during the day. So one sunny afternoon in January of 1969 when Uncle Livio dropped by to see my Dad he was surprised to find the lights on, the door locked and my Dad's pick-up truck parked out front. He knocked on the door and my Dad, having peeked around from the stock room to see who it was, answered the door. He was a good, obedient brother, so when he saw his brother, he answered the door. Uncle Livio noticed a rust-colored, oily liquid dripping from my Dad's mouth.

That morning my Dad must have gone to five separate pharmacies in town to buy the little bottles; if he had tried to purchase them all at one store, the pharmacists' suspicions would surely have been raised.

My Dad had drunk the entire five bottles of Iodine. Uncle Livio rushed him to the emergency room, my Dad not protesting at all. Auntie Gloria drove me, my brothers and Nonni Upstairs to the hospital that night. Again, we were walking through that ominous hospital and I was no less afraid than the last time we were here. My Dad was in the intensive care unit again with tubes and wires floating above his head. He smiled at us when we came through the door. I wasn't afraid of the tubes this time, so I went up to him and hugged him around the neck, and asked "Daddy are you o.k.?" His face was clammy and scratchy from the slow growth of stubble, and he smelled musty like our root cellar where Nonni Upstairs stored her homemade brandied cherries and canned fruits. He shook his head yes, and turned his face away from me.

Shortly after we arrived, a nursed brought my Dad a tray of food, which consisted of Jello (no fruit in it), and mashed potatoes with a raw egg plopped on top. I looked at that runny, gross egg and said, "Daddy, you'll get sick if you eat that raw egg. Mommy always said that eggs have to be cooked thoroughly." My father said nothing, and his face was expressionless. Nonni came over to me, gently pushed me aside and said "*State sita*" (keep quiet). I felt so sad for my Dad, and I didn't like seeing him here, so helpless and ravaged. I felt so confused.

About two days after my Dad was in the hospital, I overheard Uncle Freddy telling Nonni Upstairs that they might have to give my Dad shock treatments; I knew from all the Frankenstein movies I had seen that this was not good; I was terrified of the thought of him being strapped down to a table with electric waves charging and blasting through his body. Then I thought in a panic, "What if the doctors decide to give him a lobotomy?"

My father was spared the shock treatments, lobotomy and other primitive nostrums of the day, but he was sent back to the psychiatric ward. He was so sad, broken and defeated. He still wore however, a white shirt, his signature bow tie and his wing-tip shoes. One day we were visiting him in the large "family room," where family, friends and other visitors were able to meet with the patients. Music was playing this particular day on the stereo, the same one that my father sat by during the day, playing "Edelweiss" over and over. Today, a series of waltzes were playing. Olga Lenti, a good friend of my parents was visiting and reminiscing about what a great dancer my Dad had always been.

Olga suddenly turned to my Dad, arms stretched out and said, "Come on George." And there they were; my father gracefully glided Olga across the floor, humming to the music as he did when dancing. He waltzed her out of the room right into the hall, as my brothers and I smiled to see my father seemingly happy. All the nurses and passersby stopped to admire them; even Nonni seemed pleased this day. I followed closely behind them, joyful and proud.

My Dad's psychiatrist at the VA hospital once invited all of us—Nonni Upstairs, me, Ricci, Johnny, my father's brother Uncle Freddy and Auntie Gloria—to a therapy session with my Dad. He had a white coat on and looked very somber. I thought to myself, how's this turd going to help? I remember my poor father sitting in complete silence in the midst of loud arguing in Italian between Nonni and Uncle Freddy, whom Nonni had begun to call "*il rospo*" (the toad). Part of their argument was Nonni's claim that Nonno, Uncle Freddy and Dad's other brother Uncle Livio were taking advantage of my Dad financially ever since he became ill: "*voi altri lo derubando e vi mangiano tutti gli soldi di mei nipoti*" (you are stealing from him and eating all of my grandchildren's money). In addition to the shoe stores and construction business, my Dad and his two brothers owned a lot of property in Torrington, but I wasn't quite sure what Nonni was talking about at the time.

Another explosive issue revolved around Josepina, Nonno's young girlfriend, twenty-five years his junior, who he kept bringing to the house. Josepina looked like a grandmother trying to look young; she wore a lot of cakey make-up that was too light for her skin, a rosy-pinkish rouge that appeared slightly greasy, dark red lipstick and her hair had a cheap looking reddish-orange tint to it. I never got to know her but she always smiled at us and said hello. She really was a nonentity to me.

Nonni thought it was shameful the way he was carrying on, giving his money to her and being a bad influence on his grandchildren. She said, "*ma, come vergognoso di lei portare quella puttana a questa casa*" (how shameful of you to bring that slut to our house). Normally, I'd giggle to hear Nonni calling someone a *puttana*, but I didn't much feel like laughing this time. The psychiatrist interrupted and began to ask questions about Nonno's relationship with Josepina. As he did, he looked at me, Ricci and Johnny, and then he suddenly fixed his penetrating gaze on me and asked, "What do you think about your grandfather and this younger woman?" I panicked because all eyes were glued to me, and I was being asked to take sides: Nonni Upstairs' or Uncle Freddy's? I also resented the fact that the psychiatrist's attention regarding this question turned exclusively to me, as if I, being a young girl, found my seventy-five-year old grandfather's carrying on with a younger Italian woman somehow morally repugnant. I didn't think being a girl had anything to do with one's perceptions of moral turpitude. But, I was so scared, I just blurted out what I believed to be the truth:

"Maybe Nonno has been lonely since Nonni Next Door died, and maybe he just wants someone to keep him company." Uncle Freddy gave me a great big smile; Nonni was scowling at me. Daddy just sat there emotionless. I bowed my head down; I disclosed my feelings, but it was the wrong thing to do.

More arguing ensued and at one point I was completely shocked to see Auntie Gloria grab Nonni Upstairs by the arm, struggling to physically push her out of the room; but Nonni was not easy prey. She fought back and ripped half the dress off my aunt. Ricci and I were so disturbed by it that we walked out of the room and roamed around the halls of the hospital, trying to forget what we saw. We never said a word to each other; we just kept walking. But I just couldn't get that image out of my head: Auntie Gloria shoving my poor old grandmother.

Only two days before I was visiting her at Opperman's Drug Store in downtown Torrington: she worked the lunch counter at. When I was in Vogel Junior High, I loved walking there after school, sitting at the counter on one of the red-leathered swivel stools and having my aunt serve me a heaping helping of her freshly made coleslaw, a root-beer float, or a banana split, whichever I preferred on any particular day. I admired her toughness and her strength of spirit and soul. She was also a great comfort to my mother when she was alive. Mom entrusted Auntie Gloria with her most intimate secrets and thoughts. My aunt probably knew more about my Mom than anyone. And, next to my parents, I loved her the most.

Audrey once told me that my mother confided a lot in Auntie Gloria, telling her that her mother, Nonni Upstairs, was very controlling. That's why my Mom suddenly took a stock room job at Sears on day. I asked, "Why are you going to work, Mommy? Are we poor?" She laughed and replied, "No, Normina, now that you kids are older, I just wanted to work again. You, know, before I married your daddy, I worked all my life. I wanted to work again."

But Audrey said she needed to get out the house from the clutches of Nonni Upstairs. I thought this was odd because Nonni at least openly, never interfered with my Mom and Dad's parenting. And, Auntie Gloria never said anything to me about it. But, I always wondered about this, because Nonni was strict with us now.

Even so, this didn't justify the way my Aunt was pushing my grandmother. And why did Auntie Gloria start to violently shove Nonni only after she again accused Uncle Livio and Uncle Freddy of stealing from my father. For the first time I began to think, "Maybe Daddy is being bamboozled, and Nonni knows what's going on. She was hitting the raw nerve of truth, and they didn't want her getting in their way." All these thoughts were stirring around and around in my head and I didn't understand what was happening. This was the first and only family therapy session we had with my Dad and his psychiatrist. It was probably much more than the psychiatrist had anticipated. He probably thought that not George, but everyone else in his family belonged in the nut house.

My Uncles Freddy and Livio kicked Nonni Upstairs out of our home just before my Dad returned home from the hospital. Uncle Freddy seemed to take over as the "*BIG-ah boss-ah*" after Nonni Next Door died. He claimed that Nonni Upstairs was the cause of all the friction among the Riccucci's and he even went so far as to suggest that she was the reason for my father's suicide attempts. I was completely stunned by these accusations. I knew there were some problems in the family but didn't understand their source and certainly never thought Nonni Upstairs should be blamed for anything but protecting her three grandchildren. Granted, she was bossy and unlike my parents, hit us if we were "*cattivi*" (bad kids). But she represented safety to me. And, she was my Mom's mother, so I was very protective of her.

But, it was all arranged; my uncles informed Daddy and Nonni. I learned about this when we were visiting my Dad in the hospital one evening. Nonni started yelling at him, saying in Italian, "How could you let them kick me out like this? I have been with you since you married my daughter, and I am taking care of your children, who have no mother. Who will care for them when I am gone?" I felt sick. First, because I didn't understand why Nonni Upstairs had to leave. I thought to myself, this is her home; why should she have to leave? Daddy, do something to stop this. But at that moment my anger about Nonni leaving was eclipsed by my sympathy for my Dad. He just lay there in his hospital bed, not uttering a word. He didn't argue back, which wasn't in his nature anyway. He stared up at the ceiling muted by the ravings of my grandmother. She said goodbye and stormed out of the room. I started crying and ran to my Dad, hugging him and saying, "I'm sorry Daddy." He hugged me back and said softly, "It's o.k., don't worry. Everything will be o.k." But it wasn't.

Her son, my Uncle Bruno came to pick Nonni up. I started crying when I saw him carrying all her suitcases out to the car. I kept telling her, "Nonni please don't go; you don't have to. Daddy will let you stay." And she would say in Italian, "Norma, you just don't understand." Then she would begin to rave about my uncles stealing from my Dad. She seemed angrier about this than having to leave us. I just wanted her to stay with us and wanted my father to come home from the hospital so we could be a family again. But it had been arranged. She was to move in with her son, Bruno, and his family in Newington, Connecticut, a suburb of Hartford. My brothers and I believed that Uncle Freddy initiated the whole thing and that Uncle Livio tacitly went along with it; Bruno must have been in on it as well. Nonno may have played a part, but he was no longer present much of the time. He was spending all his time with his girlfriend, Josepina and we rarely saw him.

"Nonni, please don't go," Johnny, Ricci and I continued to cry out. She was crying in one breath and cursing my Uncle Freddy, *il rospo*, in the other. I watched from the picture window as the car slowly pulled away. When they were out of sight, I ran upstairs to her empty room, curled up on her bed and sobbed quietly into her pillow.

It was Nonni Upstairs who instilled the Italian guilt thing in me. She took the blame for adverse familial incidents. Even for her son Bruno, who I would in due time be forced to live with and would come to know as a warped, loathsome mishap. When she was pregnant with this, her third and final child, she tumbled over the front porch banister. My mother, then just 4 and Corrado, just 2, where playing a game, hiding on their mother as she was calling them in for the midday meal. They were under the front porch trying to stifle their giggles as their mother was calling for them. Over the railing she went, and Bruno was born 2 months prematurely that same day. So, when he was 16 and brought up on charges of raping a young girl, my grandmother, who thought the claims fallacious, nonetheless blamed herself for her son getting into trouble: it was her fault, "*mia culpa*," she would say because she fell when she was pregnant with him. But now, she blamed the Riccucci's.

The day after my Dad returned home from the hospital, my Uncle Freddy came to our house "for a family meeting," he said. He had the idea that it would be best for my Dad if he, Auntie Gloria and Louie moved into our house with us. He didn't have to say it directly, but I knew what he was saying: your father needs supervision so he won't hurt himself again. Before Uncle Freddy could even finish getting the words out of his mouth, my brother Johnny yelled, "we don't want you to come live with us; you already stole enough from us."

My Dad got up in a rage to take a swat at Johnny. Aside from the fact that he never spanked us, I had never seen him so angry. It surprised me but I thought, "At least he is beginning to show some interest in something." Johnny was able to escape the blow and made a run for the stairwell leading to the second floor. He sat on the steps, and every time my uncle said something about moving in, Johnny yelled out something from behind the corner, like "you ain't movin into our house." Ricci and I said nothing. We sat there and looked at my poor father who had hopelessness in his eyes. I thought, "Does Daddy really want this? Would he get better with Auntie Gloria and Uncle Freddy here?" And then, I had an awful thought, propelled by Johnny's and Nonni Upstairs' ranting: "Does

Uncle Freddy really care about Daddy, or does he just want his money?"

Not even a week had passed when my uncles checked my Dad back into the psychiatric unit of the VA hospital. They said he was depressed and needed to be under close supervision. I hated them for this. Part of me felt they were punishing my brothers and me for not letting Uncle Freddy and Auntie Gloria move in with us. They continued to admit (commit, Johnny said) my Dad to the VA's psychiatric unit periodically over the next year. With my Dad back in the hospital, my brothers and I were alone in our house. Johnny, at sixteen, was in charge of Ricci who was now thirteen, and me, twelve years old.

At some point I stopped going to meet my Dad coming home from work and stopped going to work with him. I guess I just outgrew this. I wonder if my Dad felt abandoned by me. I was twelve years old now, almost a teenager and I was just about to start junior high school. I liked hanging out more with some of the older girls in the neighborhood, like Christine Mastro and Joni Marciano. They were my brother Johnny's age—nearly four years older than me. I liked being with them because they were up on all the latest music especially the Beatles and all the popular dances. I even stopped listening to opera. "It's not cool," Chris explained.

A group of us—my brothers, Chris, Joni and my best buddy next to Ricci, Robbie who lived across the street from us and was one year younger than me—would gather at our house or Chris's to watch American Bandstand or its local version, broadcast from Hartford, Connecticut, The Brad Davis Show. We listened to the music, danced together, and made fun of those we labeled "geek," "nerd," "wierdball," "nimrod," or "queer" (which back then had no reference to sexuality).

Chris and my brother Johnny also organized talent shows, parades or raffles in the neighborhood. We sold tickets and in addition to playing the drums at any one of the talent shows, I collected the money. I had one of those silver 4-barrel coin changers that clips to a belt, the kind the Good Humor ice cream man always wore when he came down our street every day in the summer. I got it with my Bazooka Joe bubblegum comics. The coin changer set me back 300 comics, but it was worth it. I loved hearing the click of the barrel and the tinkling of the quarters, nickels, dimes and pennies being dispensed to my friends and neighbors buying tickets to our shows or raffles, where neighbors competed to win a cake or pie my Mom made for us at no charge. Johnny said I looked nerdy with the coin changer, but I felt very organized, proficient and responsible with my self-appointed task.

Chris and Joni also introduced me to the Merv Griffin and Mike Douglas Shows as well as the soap opera, *Love is a Many Splendored Thing*. I liked watching some of the famous people on Merv Griffin and Mike Douglas, like Natalie Wood, who I had a major crush on. I had seen lots of her films on The CBS Friday Night Movies, like "Sex and the Single Girl," "Penelope," and "Gypsy." I didn't always understand what was going on in the soap opera, though. But, I liked the character Laura Donnelly who, just before she took her final vows to become a Catholic nun, left the church and got married. She was way too pretty, I thought to become a nun.

When Joni and Chris started talking about make-up or boys I quickly became bored and went my separate way. Except one time, when Chris clipped Joni's diary and used a bobby pin to pick the lock. She started reading an entry that Joni had written about her boyfriend. Chris read, "We started French kissing and I became very turned on." I asked, "What's French kissing?" She said, "It's when a boy and girl kiss by sticking their tongues into each others' mouths." I said, "Yuk, that's gross. Why would anyone want to do that?" Chris, Johnny and Ricci laughed. I called them a bunch of "twurds" (my neologism, twit + turd).

Chris continued reading, "Then he started to feel my boobs, and I could feel the heat rushing through my body; I'll never wash my boobs again!" Johnny and Ricci's eyes where fixated on Chris, hanging on to her every word. I asked, "Why would the guy touch her boobs? What's that suppose to do?" Everyone cracked up again, and this time I called them *stronsi* (assholes or little shits) and walked away. "Screw them," I thought. "I'll never have a boyfriend, anyway."

But, not too long afterwards I did. Well, sort of. Chris introduced us to a game called Post Office, where a girl sits in a room in the dark and a boy goes into the "post office," sits beside her and delivers a kiss. Then the lights are turned on and you learn who kissed whom. Since my brothers were playing I asked, "What if I'm the girl sitting and one of my brothers comes in?" Chris said, "We'll make sure that doesn't happen." Still a little resistant to the game I said, "If I'm going to play, I don't want anyone sticking their stupid tongue down my throat." Everyone laughed and Chris responded, "Don't be such a big baby." Well, that did it; no one calls me a baby. So I played along.

I was sitting on our living room sofa; next thing I know a boy was sitting next to me and he kissed me fast on the lips; we both giggled. The lights when on and it was Robbie. Chris was laughing hysterically, so I know she orchestrated this little jig. But instead of anger toward Chris, I suddenly became very shy around Robbie. I actually liked kissing him, as long as our lips where tightly closed. We kissed a few times after that, but it soon lost its novelty for both of us. Anyway, Robbie was my pal, and I much preferred riding bikes and playing basketball and baseball with him than kissing.

Even when my Dad was home from the hospital, Johnny was still in charge, because my Dad was oblivious to all our doings. Ricci and I nonetheless continued with our shenanigans. I remember taking some very risky liberties with our driving privileges.

Ricci and I were obsessed with cars. Our cousin Georgie, Livio's son owned a red 1962 Corvette Stingray convertible with white leather bucket seats. It was about his fourth; he was forever cracking them up and his father kept replacing them with new ones. Georgie occasionally took Ricci and me for long rides with him. Our two small butts fit perfectly in the passenger's side bucket seat; knowing Georgie's penchant for driving fast and getting into accidents, Johnny made us buckle our seatbelt.

Ricci and I also made certain we were with our Dad whenever he dropped by the used car shop on Main Street in Torrington owned by the Riccucci brothers. As he talked business with the manager he and my uncles hired to run the place, Ricci and I would run around from car to car, sit inside and pretend we were driving. It was so exhilarating. And, I thought everyone shared our obsession, but I soon learned I was wrong. One day, I stunned by den mother and friends in my Girl Scout troop when, to earn my hobby badge, I brought in my collection of Matchbox cars. I had them arrayed systematically and neatly in their matrix-like cubbyholes in my Matchbox vinyl-leatherette carrying case. My favorite was the white 1963 Jaguar XK-E with the tiny doors that opened. Bobby, one of my classmates traded it for my red with white hardtop 1957 Chevy Bel Air. It was a clunky little car, and I didn't know why he would trade it for his cool Jaguar, but I didn't ask. As I proudly displayed the case and its contents, I glanced over at my den mother, whose eyes were glazed over and her mouth gapping; she was completely stupefied. The other girl scouts were pointing at me, giggling.

It was often the case, when my father wasn't home, nor was Uncle Freddy, Auntie Gloria or Nonno, that Ricci and I would sneak out to our Oldsmobile Super 88, our pick-up truck, or the Scout Jeep and take turns driving up and down the street. For a long time, no one seemed to catch on. Not even Johnny, who would have tattled on us in a flash. One of my best ideas came to me when no one was home and both the pick-up and Scout were parked in front of our house.

Uncle Freddy's driveway was pretty wide; at least three cars could fit side-by-side. Directly across the street from his driveway was Mr. and Mrs. Crane's, which was wide enough to accommodate at least two vehicles. So, with Ricci in the pick-up and me in the yellow, three-on-the floor Scout, we backed up into the Crane's driveway with our rear bumpers butted up against their garage door. After making certain there was no oncoming traffic, Ricci and I took turns yelling out, "Ready, on your mark, get set, go!" We'd peel out and race across the street into my uncle's driveway till we reached his set of garage doors.

We downshifted whenever we could, which in our minds was one of the coolest things about driving. What a blast it was! We were fearless perhaps reckless. This went on for about a half an hour until our prudent, risk-averse sides realized that an adult would soon be home; so we parked the Jeep and truck where we found them.

The last time we snuck off in the Super 88 was when we mistakenly thought no one but my father was home. Daddy had just returned once again from a stay in the psychiatric ward of the Veteran's hospital in Hartford and was taking a nap; Ricci and I grabbed the keys from the kitchen table and made a run for the car. We took turns driving up and down the street. Ricci was pulling into the driveway to let me take my turn at the wheel, when who do we see standing there with steam coming out of his ears, Uncle Freddy. I said, "oh, oooooh, we're going to get it now." He intimidated me, especially because he used to beat his son Louie with a belt; and poor Louie was always getting into trouble. Uncle Freddy started yelling at us, "What the hell is the matter with you kids! Don't you know you can get hurt, or hurt other people? It's against the law, too!" As if that would even scare or deter us. He reached into the car and pulled the keys from the ignition and marched into our house to my father's bedroom. Uncle Freddy proceeded to rant and rave at my Dad, telling him how irresponsible he was as a father. My father was lying on his back, hands clasped behind his head, staring up at the ceiling; he never uttered a word. I stood there, looking at my poor father; I felt real bad for him and wanted to kick myself for what we had done. It was this sight and not my uncle's protestations, which led me to never again sneak off with the car, truck or Jeep.

I think this is when I began, for the first time, to feel a deep sense of acrimony toward not just my uncles but also my entire family. Here we were, living alone for the longest time, sometimes with but often without my father, and never once did Uncle Freddy, Auntie Gloria, Nonno, Uncle Livio or Auntie Pauline come to check in on my brothers and me. Never once did they invite us over to share a meal with them. And why was their front door always locked now? What had we done to make them hate us this much? Where was everyone? So, what right did Uncle Freddy have to belittle and lecture my father about parental responsibilities? "He doesn't give a crap about us," I thought.

The only person who ever looked in on us was my godmother from across the street, Robbie's Mom, Anne Favali, whom I adored. I was extremely close to Anne, as I called her all my life. Ever since I can remember, Anne and her entire family called me Normie. Anne was my godmother at confirmation. The Sacrament of Confirmation was the rite of passage. It admits us to the church as adults. I think it was another way to ensure our commitment to going to church every Sunday and putting money in those little envelopes and dropping them in the collection basket during mass.

Anne lived directly across the street from us in a two-story stone house. In addition to Robbie, she had a daughter Elysie (who we called LEE-see), who was a good 11 years older than him. I never knew Anne's husband, Dino, who worked on the Thomaston dam. He died when Robbie was a baby. He was buried alive by stone, gravel and dirt in the construction of the dam. Anne never talked much about him, nor did Robbie, who never knew his own father. I felt sorry for Robbie, because he didn't have a Dad. It wasn't fashionable to be a single Mom then, but Anne never remarried. She worked most of her life as a waitress in order to support herself and her children. I loved and admired her for her kindness, independence, strength, and self-assuredness. If there was a safety net now for my brothers and me, it was Anne, who regularly checked in on us, coming over almost every afternoon to make certain we were doing o.k., and often took us for rides in her jet-black, three-on-the floor, Chevy Impala convertible. She also invited us to her house for dinner. I always wanted to say, "Yes, we want to eat at your house. What are you fixin?" But, Johnny always quickly replied, "Thank you, Anne, but we'll eat at our house."

These days, we were eating a lot of frozen food—pot pies, Swanson's frozen dinners, and frozen pizzas. And they constipated me. I really missed my Mom's and Nonni Upstairs' cooking. Now, I wished I had paid more attention to them cooking. I remember staying home sick from school one day. Ricci stayed home with me so I wouldn't be alone. For some reason, he decided to make bacon and eggs for breakfast. He cooked the bacon and eggs together, in the same pan at the same time. We ate raw bacon and burnt eggs.

Staring at the mushy meatloaf and neatly compartmentalized vegetables—tasteless mashed potatoes and tiny shriveled up plastic peas —in my aluminum T.V. dinner tray, I thought back on meals, especially around the holidays, that my Mom and grandmothers had once prepared.

I have a very clear memory of the first and last time I went grocery shopping with my brother Johnny. We had a grocery cart full of prepared and frozen foods. As the checker was ringing us out, she asked, and not jokingly, "Are you having a party or something?"

Johnny politely responded, "No." I smiled as if she were joking and cringed when I realized she wasn't; I tried to hide behind Johnny. She must have been thinking, "Why do they have so many frozen pizzas and pot pies?"

I couldn't poop. Weeks would go by and I couldn't take a dump to save my life. I would panic during these times, sitting for a long period of time on the pot, just straining and grunting like an old lady. Was I going to bloat up and die from backed-up human waste? I was eventually able to poop, and what a relief. I must have been the only twelve-year old with hemorrhoids.

My poor father, who was accustomed to my Mom's home-cooked, specially-prepared meals for his ulcerated stomach, sat and ate those frozen Swanson dinners with us. He never complained.

Only once did I ever hear my Dad raise his voice to one of his brothers. Since there was no one to take us camping in the summers, my Dad sold the trailer for about $800 bucks. When my Uncle Freddy found out that my Dad sold the trailer for far less than its value of $1500, he started to reprimand him. I was startled when I heard my Dad yell back, "Don't tell me what to do. Who's gonna take my kids camping now?" And then I was shaken to hear him say, "You took their grandmother away, and now they have no one. I can't take care of my kids on my own. What am I gonna do?" It frightened me because it finally registered in my head that my Dad wasn't going to give up.

Act III. Scene 3.
Suicido!

("*Suicide*," from Ponchielli's *La Gioconda)*

It was raining hard and I didn't have my raincoat on. When the school bus dropped me off at the end of my street, I began to run, thinking, like an idiot that I wouldn't get that wet if I ran. Our house was about an eighth of a mile from the bus stop, which was at the corner of our road and Main Street.

As I got closer to our house, I caught a glimpse through my straggly, rain-soaked hair of Mr. LaPorta's big black hearse. It looked like the same one that had carried my mother's dead body two years earlier. It still had the small rear window framed with laced curtains. There were several other big black cars parked in front of our house, including a Torrington police car. I panicked as I ran closer to the house and I began crying and hyperventilating. When I entered our side of the house, I saw my Auntie Pauline standing in the kitchen, vacuously staring out of the back window. Ricci was sitting on the living room sofa, whimpering.

I asked him, "Is he dead?"

Ricci cried, "He killed himself."

I could no longer feel my legs and arms; my body dropped to the floor, my History and English books crashing down next to me. I began sobbing uncontrollably. Uncle Livio's wife my Auntie Pauline, unable to comfort either Ricci or me just stood there with a blank look on her face. Ricci began crying harder and we both just walked around the house in circles, scared and trembling.

Johnny should have been home by now, but he wasn't. "Where's Johnny?" I asked. "He's driving Dennis home," Ricci told me. They were planning to study together at our house, but when they arrived and learned what had happened, Johnny's first instinct was to get Dennis out of there. Ricci was left alone with Auntie Pauline.

I wondered why Auntie Pauline was sent over to our side of the house to be with us. She was never our closest aunt, and was somewhat aloof and indifferent. I later learned that she was intentionally sent over because no one else wanted to be with us. I really wanted, *needed* the comfort of my Auntie Gloria, whom I felt safe with and loved almost as much as I loved my own mother. But she would not come to us. The entire time she remained next door at Nonno's side of the house. The chasm in the family had gotten so thick and impermeable, that even in death, the Riccucci's would not come to our aid.

At one point, a Torrington police officer came over to our side of the house and asked my sobbing brother and me, "Did any of youse find a note or somethin'?" We didn't respond, because we didn't know what he meant. I told him, looking up into his eyes, searching for some comfort, "I'm really scared." And, for some unapparent reason, he grabbed me by both of my wrists, practically lifted my body off the floor, shook me and said, "You know, I lost my father, too. Just think about that."

He released my wrists and I fell backwards, continuing to look into his dark, expressionless eyes. He walked away, and went back into Nonno's side of the house. I stood there for a minute or two, with tears streaming down my face, trying to figure out what the hell he was talking about. What did he mean, and what had I done wrong? Did my grandfather or Uncle Freddy tell him that we were bad kids?

I'll never forget those many years later when I saw *The Tracy Thurman Story* on T.V. It was a true story that took place in Torrington and it showed how stupid, irresponsible and callous some of the Torrington police officers were. Tracy Thurman was a victim of espousal abuse and even a court order wasn't able to keep her estranged husband away from her. When Torrington police officers were called to the scene where her husband was brutalizing her, they not only took their time responding to the call, but then, when they arrived, they quiescently stood by while her husband stabbed, maimed, and left her for dead. Tracy Thurman eventually won a multimillion-dollar lawsuit against the Torrington Police Department; I felt a deep sense of gratification and vindication.

Johnny eventually came home, and time just seemed to stand still. Johnny said, "We're going to Nonni." I think Auntie Pauline was relieved, because she was now off the hook and could leave the flotsam that was us. Johnny instructed us to grab some clothes, because he would be driving us to my Aunt Mary's and Uncle Bruno's, where Nonni Upstairs was now living.

I asked, "Why can't we go to Auntie Gloria's?" Johnny said "We're going to Nonni." I guess I still didn't understand, or didn't want to know why the Riccucci's wanted nothing to do with us.

I don't remember being in the car or driving; it was still raining out, but warm for a day in February. I only remember looking up at the Avon Mountain, feeling scared and bewildered. Johnny first stopped at Lucia and Compare's pizza house. It was very comforting, a gesture that I will never forget. Lucia sat us in a booth and brought us each a big bowl of *broddo* with *pastina*. I took small sips of it, but felt too disoriented to eat. I kept asking Lucia, "What happened to my father?" but she would not tell; tell me how he had done it this time.

We loaded in the car again and Johnny drove us to Newington, where my grandmother, Aunt Mary, Uncle Bruno and cousins Little Johnny and Nancy awaited us. I felt awash in desperation, and I did *not* want to be going to Uncle Bruno's house. I just wanted to go home and have everything be okay again.

It felt like déjà vu at my father's wake; I was standing in the vestibule crying and trembling. I told my Aunt Mary, who was standing next to me, "I'm scared." I was afraid of seeing my dead father lying in a casket. She put her arm around me and said, "There's nothing to be afraid about." I started to hyperventilate and it was Nonni Upstairs who came to me and talked me down into a state of normal breathing. The door opened, and there was Mr. LaPorta; he appeared to wearing the same clothes as he wore for my Mom's wake. He even had the tiny white carnation placed neatly in his button hole. I thought, "Does he only have one suit?"

This time when we walked into the flower filled room where my Dad was, the casket was closed; there was an American flag draped over it. I asked Auntie Mary, "Where's my Dad and why is the casket closed?" She turned to me and matter-of-factly said, "Your father shot himself in the head; half of his face was blown away." If I had anything in my stomach, I would have retched it up. The words kept stinging, pounding over and over in my head.

"He shot himself."

While we were sitting next to the casket, I felt as though I was in a trance, trying to trace and retrace my father's footsteps on that fatal day on February 10th. How he must have walked catatonically down the stairs into his father's basement and over to the beautiful wooden rifle cabinet with the long glass door, framed in honey-hued oak wood. My grandfather had made the cabinet when he first came to this country. It stored Nonno's five hunting rifles and shotguns; it had no lock or key because no one but my grandfather ever used these guns. Ricci, Louie and I often peered at them through the glass door, but we knew better than to ever lay a finger on the cabinet, because Nonno would know. He told us that he dusted it for fingerprints.

Detached and despondent, my father must have arbitrarily selected a shotgun, removed it and loaded it. I didn't even know he could use a gun because he never went hunting with Nonno. I thought, "He peeled potatoes during the war, so how did he know how to shot one of these things?" "Daddy, why don't you ever go hunting with Nonno," I asked one day. He fibbed, "I don't know how to shoot a gun." The pieces would eventually fit, once I learned about his experiences in Normandy. Did he feel guilty for not having his head blown off as many of the soldiers did?

Dad must have made a conscious choice to shoot himself in his father's bedroom so that none of his children would find him in a pool of his own blood.

What was going through his mind when he gently placed his finger or thumb (which was it?) on the trigger. Was he crying? Was he scared? Was he thinking about me, Ricci and Johnny? Mommy? Was the barrel of the gun pressed up against his temple or was it in his mouth? What happened in that split second when the gun went off and it made impact with my father's flesh?

IN HIS HEAD.

"Why in the head?" I kept repeating over and over again in my mind. "Why not in the stomach, chest or more fittingly, the heart?"

I felt myself drifting away.

I wanted to see my father's body, but knew it was impossible. I felt, at least, that in my own way, I had the chance to say goodbye to him. Two nights before he died, I remember standing in the hallway, hugging him goodnight. In our family, one didn't get up in the morning, go to bed at night, enter or exit the house without kissing each other. I kissed his stubbly cheek and said, "You are the best Daddy in the whole world; I love you very much." He didn't seem to want to let me go. He said, "I love you too, *bambola*." I wanted to add, "Please don't leave us, Daddy," but couldn't quite get the words out. I knew that at some level, my Dad was ashamed about his previous suicide attempts, and I didn't want to remind him of them, so, I kept my big mouth shut.

Johnny, Ricci and I sat up front in the funeral parlor, as we did when my mother died, just off to the side of my father's casket. I just hoped that it was satin-lined, like my Mom's was.

I thought, as I looked at the casket, "Now you are at peace, Daddy. Now you are with Mommy."

But then a sudden wave of panic came over me. I remembered Sister Zita lecturing in catechism one afternoon about suicide.

"It is a mortal sin against God, who gave us the gift of life," she said in her dogmatic, pedantic way.

"Those who commit suicide would burn in hell," she bellowed. I couldn't bear the thought that my parents may not be reunited in heaven. It was then and there that I came to the conclusion that there could not be a hell; maybe a purgatory, but no hell.

How could a loving, forgiving God be so spiteful and cruel as to banish souls to an inferno full of puss, guts, puke, vermin, and ubiquitous shit for all eternity? I thought to myself.

No, it was not possible. This had to be another one of Sister Zita's ploys to scare us little innocent pixies into complete and unequivocal devotion to God.

People streamed in and out, shaking our hands and kneeling and praying in front of the casket. What a horrible ritual this was, I was thinking to myself, and vowed to myself that I would never, ever go to another wake again in my life.

I kept glancing over at my Auntie Gloria, who was sitting in the second row with Uncle Freddy, Auntie Pauline and Uncle Livio. They were physically removed from my brothers and me. Every time I looked at her she diverted her eyes, mostly downwards. She did not want to make eye contact with me, and this was crushing; ever since that day my father killed himself, Auntie Gloria and everyone else on my Dad's side of the family kept their distance from us and I still didn't fully know why.

This time, there wasn't the fleet of black limousines as there was at my mother's funeral. There was no remaining adult who was willing to take the time and care to tenderly plan the ritual of burial, as my father had done for my mother two years before. It was a simple ceremony, and he was buried without any of the fanfare accorded to my mother.

For a long time afterwards, I have this recurring dream that I am the one who finds him. The dream begins with me walking slowly down a dimly-lit corridor which opens up into a room radiantly bright with sun beams. I tentatively walk through the door and into the room only to see my father lying in a thick, gooey pool of his own blood; half of his head is missing, completely blown away. It is the darkest, reddest blood I have ever seen; it has splattered everywhere. There is no gun to be found. He is still alive. I kneel down beside him, haltingly lift his head, which, through some slow-moving, surreal sequence, is now fully intact, and place it in my lap. I scream for help. "Oh, please God, don't let him die." Only no one hears my plea because the room no longer has a door, or any windows. The sunlight continues to swath the room but its source remains a mystery to me. I look around the room searching for something, for someone to help me, give me a clue as to what to do. He looks at me, his eyes deep and sorrowful. He says nothing but his contemplative eyes beseech me to let him go. The dream always ends here, with me waking in a cold sweat, screaming.

Act III. Scene 4.
Per Me Ora Fatale

("*For Me the Hour is Fatal*,"
from Verdi's *Il Travatore*)

We were to live with my Aunt Mary and Uncle Bruno because they had become our legal guardians. In his last will and testament, my Dad had named his brother Livio as our guardian but my uncle refused to take us. Some sort of arrangement, which involved money—lots according to my grandmother—led to the appointment of Auntie Mary and Uncle Bruno as our trustees.

Aunt Mary and Uncle Bruno were my baptismal godparents. Growing up, I loved my Aunt Mary because she was so much fun to be around. She'd be talking seriously one minute, and the next minute she'd break into a Carol Burnett-like soft-shoe tap routine that would crack everyone up. Her kooky, screwball antics provided an unending supply of laughs to all of us, except Uncle Bruno. He always scared me a little, because he was so stern, serious and forbidding; he was incapable of laughing or smiling. I was always very polite around him but the discomfort he caused made me stay clear of him.

Now, I dreaded having to live with my aunt and uncle at 96 Hawley Street, as I would come to know that wretched house. I was resistant and reluctant, despite the fact that my grandmother was living there. I wanted to go back to Greenridge Road and live with Auntie Gloria. When I said this to Nonni, she said very coolly, "Don't you know that your aunt and uncle don't want to have anything to do with you three kids?"

I asked, "But, why? What did we do?"

And she repeated a few times, in her perdurable, sarcastic way, "Eh, why? Eh, why?" And went on to say in Italian, "Because your Uncle Freddy is a *rospo* (toad), and a *ladro* (thieve). He and your grandfather stole everything your mother and father ever worked for. They certainly don't want you around as a constant reminder to their heinous deeds; it might weigh on their conscience, if any of them have one. Wait and see, one day, they'll deny your very existence."

I still didn't understand. Maybe I just didn't want to understand. Maybe I just didn't want to know the truth about my family, whom I so loved and adored.

Johnny was lucky. Aunt Mary agreed to let him finish out his junior year of high school in Torrington. Newington High School didn't have the classes he needed, so he would have been sent back to sophomore level classes. Even Aunt Mary saw the stupidity in this and so she allowed Johnny to return to Torrington. Mary made arrangements for Johnny to move in at least through the end of his school year with Uncle Livio and Auntie Pauline, *la Americana*.

This gave me an idea. Despite what Nonni told me about Uncle Freddy, I called my Aunt Gloria about a week after I moved to Newington. I said, "Hi, Auntie Gloria. It's me, Norma. Can I come to visit you?" There was silence at the other end of the line for what seemed to be an eternity. And then, through a cracked voice which seemed to be holding back tears, she said, "No Norma, I don't think that's a good idea." My heart dropped. I felt such a deep sense of confusion and anguish, but at 13 years old, I was still not emotionally mature enough to know what to do. So, I started to cry, and I said, "O.K., then. Bye Auntie Gloria." I didn't know what else to say. It would be the last time we'd ever talk to one another.

Several weeks later, I decided to telephone my Uncle Livio to see if I could live with him and Auntie Pauline. Johnny was there so maybe I had a chance. "Uncle Livio, can I come and live with you?" He mumbled something like, "What the hell are you talkin' about. I got Johnny here for a few months, but I can't take you in after all that's happened" and then hung up the phone. I still didn't know *what* had happened. Was it the money as Nonni maintained?

I didn't bother to ask Nonno if I could live with him. I didn't want to because I was never that close to him. He would have said no anyway. He blamed my brothers and me for my Dad's death. One day when my brothers and I returned to our house to collect some of our belongings, Nonno came across our front lawn and yelled in Italian, "You were rotten kids and it's your fault that your father killed himself (*la colpa di vostra*)." For a long time afterwards, I believed him—believed that if we were better children, that my father would still be alive.

My last hope was my godmother, Anne Favali: "Can I come to live you?" Why does the phone seem to go dead every time I ask this question? She said that she would love to have me live with her, but thought it best if I lived with my grandmother and aunt and uncle. "Normie, why don't you want to live with them?" she asked. I couldn't tell her that I was afraid of my uncle and what he might do to me.

We were cramped in that small, dingy-gray, clapboard house without any exterior shutters. My aunt and uncle slept in the master bedroom on the first floor; Ricci and Little Johnny shared a room on the second floor and Nonni, their daughter Nancy and I shared the other room on the second floor. Their other daughter Claudia was married and living in an apartment with her husband, *il divorziato* (the divorced one, as Nonni continued to refer to him as). I slept with Nonni in her double bed, and I felt very safe there, despite the fact that she smelled like Ponds cold cream and her snoring distracted me from the nightmares I had of my Dad, and the constant feelings of guilt for having abandoned him, the continued longing for Mom, and the fear that Bruno would catch me off guard. Most of the night I lay awake staring at the old faded brown wallpaper or the window, whose thin-yellowed shade could not eclipse the fractured beams of moonlight from streaming in.

It was very tumultuous at 96 Hawley Street. There was constant bickering between Nonni, and my aunt and uncle about who possessed the right to parent Ricci and me. It was just one more thing in a long line of fractious ordeals between Auntie Mary and Nonni. They never got along very well. They only tolerated each other while my parents were alive, but after they died, the two returned to their mutual dislike for one another.

Nonni never liked Mary because, for one thing, she was pregnant with her first child, Claudia, when she married my uncle. My uncle was forced to marry her and my grandmother believed that Mary deliberately entrapped him. My grandmother would not, *did* not attend their wedding, and was not happy that my mother did.

A secondary reason Nonni disliked Mary was because my aunt is *Siciliana*. Italians from regions other then Sicily have traditionally and historically looked down upon Sicilians. This is not what children of my generation believe. But Italians of my grandparents' generation thought of Sicilians as lower-class philistines, completely amoral and corrupt. After all, they would say, the Mafioso had its roots in *Sicilia*. And, there was some truth to this, at least in Mary's case. Her brother Louie Failla would stop by 96 Hawley Street every six months or so with piles of new women's and men's clothing. Shirts, blouses, pants, slacks, jackets, all neatly hung on narrow wooden hangers, protected by the same kind of plastic wrap that dry-cleaners used. Louie was selling the clothes for "real cheap, a good bargain" he'd proclaim. I remember the first time Louie showed up with his stash. I asked my aunt, "Where did all this stuff come from and why is it so cheap?" My aunt said, "My brother is in the wholesale business." But my cousin Nancy quickly shot back, "Ma, this is stolen stuff; he got it off the warehouse trucks unloading in New York City." My aunt just shrugged her shoulders and kept pulling blouses out for her and shirts for Bruno. It all looked like crap to me so I never bought anything. I would learn years later that Louie was indicted on racketeering charges (the conspiracy to murder charges were dropped for lack of evidence). The court papers referred to him as "a low level Mafioso," a member of the Patriarca crime family from Connecticut. He was convicted and served several years in federal prison.

I recall one Saturday evening when Ricci, my cousin Johnny and I were watching the Jackie Gleason Show on television. We particularly loved "The Honeymooners" especially when Ralph bellowed, "You're going to the moon, Alice," or "Pow, right in the kisser!" My grandmother was in the kitchen unloading the dishwasher and Mary and Bruno were sitting at the kitchen table drinking coffee.

Nonni yelled out that it was time for Ricci and me to go to bed; it was past nine o'clock. "Norma! Ricci! *Andate a letto*," she called out.

Of course, as typical young teenagers wanting to stay up late on a Saturday night, Ricci and I began to whine, "Oh, do we have to?"

My uncle roared back, "They don't have to go to bed yet; it's early."

My grandmother barked back, "You take care of your kids, I'll take care of mine."

My uncle shot back in his typical trite, churlish and unenlightened way, "As long as they're living under my roof, I'll tell them what they can and can't do."

My grandmother screamed as she continued to unload the dishwasher, "They're *my* kids and *I'll* tell them what to do." She must have been holding at least a half dozen white dinner plates at the time, which she proceeded to crash down onto the kitchen floor. The noise was so loud and jolting, it even scared Mary and Bruno's black and white sheep dog, Tammy.

I ran into the kitchen and uttered apprehensively, "Ricci and I are going to bed now." I happened to glance over at my aunt, who was trying to hide her cocky smile behind her coffee mug. She seemed gratified, almost avenged whenever Uncle Bruno fought with his mother.

Bruno looked at me and said, "Go back in that living room and watch T.V."

A cacophonous shouting match between Nonni and Uncle Bruno ensued. As I walked upstairs to bed, I could still hear them screaming at each other in Italian.

Nonni, who had originally suspected only the Riccucci's of ripping my father off, now had reason to believe that her son and daughter-in-law had some part in the deception and depredation.

After the death of my Dad, our house was pillaged and plundered by marauding family members. Things just mysteriously disappeared; even the several thousands dollars in cash that my father kept in the house for emergencies or other contingencies (there were no ATM machines back then). My grandmother eventually learned that her own son and daughter-in-law had benefitted from the raiding. My grandmother mostly blamed not her son, but the bad seed, the "*Siciliana*," who, in the true spirit of double entendre, she began referring to as "*quel buco nero*," the black hole.

Everything started to unravel when my grandmother, who still had this Depression-style mentality of socking cash away in her mattress, was soon finding small sums of money missing. She confronted Aunt Mary about the missing cash, but was summarily dismissed by her as being a senile old woman. It seemed inconceivable that my aunt would stoop to such cheap, contemptible behavior, and at the time I did not believe it possible. It was years later, after I got my first job, that I discovered that Mary really was a *ladra* (thief) and a *bugiarda* (liar). The meager earnings that I was squirreling away in an envelope in my underwear drawer began to disappear and I figured out that it was no other than my aunt. What little I had was being filched. "What kind of person would steal from a teenager?" I thought to myself.

The fighting between my grandmother and aunt became so intolerable to them both, that Nonni was asked to leave, or kicked out as I thought of it. Nonni knew it was best, only she assumed that when she moved out, Ricci and I would move out with her. But my Aunt had another scheme in mind.

It wasn't that my Aunt wanted us, although she did benefit financially by having us. Not only did she receive sizable monthly social security checks—"survivors' benefits," they were called—written out to Ricci and me, but she also had access to our inheritance, which I learned years later had been depleted and severely ravaged before my Dad even died. My aunt was forever contacting Mr. Owen, our trustee, at Connecticut Bank and Trust, saying that she needed him to cut a check for Norma and Ricci because they needed this or that. The "that" turned out to be a trip for Mary and Bruno to Italy, a new car, aluminum siding for 96 Hawley Street and a bunch of other stuff never intended for Ricci or me. I wonder how many times Mr. Owen fell for that old ruse.

The real issue here was power—my aunt had to be in control and she wasn't about to let my grandmother get one up on her. I remember my aunt barking out the command, "Ricci and Norma will be living here with us." She and Nonni began to scream loudly at one another. Nonni said, "They are my kids and they're coming to live with me. You don't care about them; you only care about their money." Then, I yelled as loudly as I could, "I want to go and live with Nonni." And Mary looked at me, her face so distorted by anger it made me recoil, and said, "I'll put you in an orphanage before that will ever happen. Don't you know that I and your uncle have legal custody of you kids until you turn eighteen?" Nonni yelled back at her, "you're such an evil shit, you would do something malicious like that." I was so stunned I didn't know what to say. Mary just turned back to my grandmother and they continued their screaming match.

The next few days I kept begging Nonni not to leave. But she said that she had no choice. She was being forced to go by her "*figlio con nessuna spina dorsale*" (spineless son) and "*quella puttana di una zia che lei ha*" (that slut of an aunt you have). She tried to initiate custody proceedings, but a sleazy Hartford-based lawyer, colluding with Mary and Bruno, told Nonni that the adoption laws in the state of Connecticut precluded someone of her age from adopting children. I would later learn that there is no such provision nor was there ever such a provision in Connecticut's adoption laws. And one day when I came home from school, Nonni was gone.

The thought of her being gone brought on a flood of anxieties. I missed the days when I was a kid and the only thing I had to worry about was getting spanked. My biggest fear was my uncle. "With Nonni gone, who will protect me from him?" I thought. It won't be safe for me now at 96 Hawley Street. What will I do?

"And how could her own son kick her out?" I kept asking myself. It pained me to think of my grandmother, who had been surrounded by her loving family for so long, and who had experienced the utter misery of losing a daughter, then her home, would be living alone in a small flat in Hartford, where her life's journey in America all began. She was seventy-four years old. "Will she ever find peace in this life?" I asked myself. Nonni was also the strongest link to my past. Everything about her reminded me of home, my parents, love and safety. My heart was breaking.

Mary attempted to prevent Ricci and me who now answered only to Richard or Rich, from having any contact with either our grandmother or even our brother Johnny, who was still in Torrington finishing high school. My aunt never said outright that we couldn't visit or communicate with Johnny or Nonni. She had more cunning ways of letting us know she disapproved. If I communicated with either of them by phone, she ridiculed or badgered me incessantly and concussively. My spineless, wimp of an Uncle stopped talking to his own mother because he succumbed to Mary's ruthless harassing and browbeating.

I in turn reacted adversely not so much to her responses, but to her inappropriate, flagrant attempts to keep me from seeing or communicating with my own grandmother and oldest brother. My grandmother's sole purpose for the remainder of her life was to ensure the best interests of her daughter's children and to keep the three of us together as a family. Aunt Mary only sought to drive a wedge between us and I was going to do everything I could to prevent her from succeeding.

So, I started to sneak around, making clandestine phone calls to Nonni or secretly taking the bus into Hartford to visit her. She lived in a flat on New Britain Avenue, just off of Franklin Avenue, the small Italian enclave that survived gentrification and the economic developments that pushed all the ethnic groups out of Hartford. She lived on the third floor of a decaying brownstone that was built in the early 1900s, probably by Italian-immigrant stonemasons like her husband. There was no elevator but fortunately the interior was still in pretty good shape. The rich cherry-wood staircase had heavy, think banisters, and the glossy varnished hard wood floors were always spotless, because Signorina Rosina, the

Italian immigrant from Calabria who owned the building with her now deceased husband was always sweeping and dusting the floors, despite her hunched back ("*è gobba*," Nonni would say). There were no runners, so I made certain to tell Nonni, "Be careful going up an down the stairs, 'cause they're slippery."

I loved Nonni's flat, because it reminded me of my home on Greenridge Road in Torrington. When Nonni discovered that the Riccucci's, Bruno and Mary were raiding our home, she hired a moving truck and collected most of my parents' furniture from the house. She had my parents' sofa, the matching pale green olive armchairs, a wooden rocking chair, our Silverstone Stereo Hi-Fi, and my parent's bedroom furniture. The red leather rocking chair—the one my Mom and I used to sit in—had to be left behind; there was no room for it in the flat, Nonni told me. Even if my parents' furniture hadn't been there, Nonni's flat felt like home to me anyway.

I always tried to time my visits around noon. Now that she was on her own, my grandmother reverted back to her old customs, eating her main meal around noontime. And, except for pasta, everything was homemade, including her most wonderful *panini*. One of my favorite meals was her fried chicken. She whacked the chicken into small parts and then rolled it in flour and batter; her batter was of the same type used for veal parmesan, so, it was thick and flavorful. With the chicken, she served another of my favorites—*fiore di zucca* (fried squash flowers or blossoms); fried, sliced zucchini and homemade *patati friti* (or Italian fries). I think what made it all taste so good was that Nonni reused her frying oil two or three times, and she fried everything in the same oil. A fresh garden salad, a homemade *panino* and a glass of red wine accompanied the meal.

My grandmother was the best cook. My aunt was also pretty good at cooking, but she prepared food more along the lines of Italian Nouvelle. She'd watch cooking shows such as the Galloping Gourmet and the French Chef, and then experiment by adapting the recipes to an Italian genre. Baked stuffed mushroom caps, *alla Romana*. And, no one was allowed to cook at 96 Hawley Street except my aunt; my uncle forbade anyone else from preparing *his* meals. My grandmother often referred to me as "*la Cenerentola*," (Cinderella) because my aunt had me doing everything else: the washing, cleaning, and ironing.

One time during lunch, Nonni turned on the Hi-Fi to listen to the Saturday Met broadcast. Beverly Sills was performing in Verdi's *La Traviata*. I got up from the table and turned it off. She asked, "What are you doing? Don't you want to hear the broadcast?" I told her, "No, I just want to talk." I didn't want to lie to her, to tell her that I wasn't yet ready to reintroduce opera into my life. It was still too painful; it reminded me of the death of my parents and all the bad shit that went along with it. I can sometimes even hear Nonni's moan of grief-stricken pain, "*È morta?*", when she learned her daughter was dead. "No, I don't want to be reminded," I told myself.

After lunch, we'd either play cards (*scopa* or gin rummy) in her small, screened-in porch in the rear of her flat, or just talk. Sometimes, I would go into her bedroom to the place where she kept all of her sepia photos that spanned her life from about the time she was married to until just before her daughter, my Mom, died. Some were neatly arranged in wonderfully worn tan Italian photo albums, but most were piled orderly in those handsome old tins that were once filled with colorful, sweet Christmas ribbon candy. Nonni would narrate as we flipped through the old photos and retell the stories of when she was born, how she came to America, how my Mom loved Italy, what my Mom's friends were like: Here's your mother with her friend Palma, who moved back to Italy with her husband because they hated it here in America. "*Brava*," she would say. And look how very stylish your mother was. She loved to dress up, and she made a lot of her clothes. Then, without even glancing over at me, she would invariably say while shaking her head, "and look at you, still wearing your 'rubber hose.' You took after the Riccucci's (*i contadini*)." I would just chuckle and continue to look at the pictures.

Once, I asked my grandmother, "don't you get lonely here all by yourself?" She said she didn't have time to think about such things; it would not come to any good. But she did say that she missed "*la sua Mamma e voi altri ragazzi*" (I miss your mother and you kids). But then she shared an anecdote she picked up from her good friend Guiditta Bacconi: "*Meglio soli, che mal' accompagniati.*" Roughly, this means, you're better off alone than with bad company or a rotten companion. To this day, I still believe the truth in this.

My grandmother and I would also go for long, meandering walks, sometimes through the well-manicured grounds of Trinity College, with its architecturally aesthetic, Anglican edifices. My favorite building was the massive Gothic chapel, the crowning centerpiece of this medieval-looking liberal arts college. Sometimes we would sit on a bench for long periods of time and listen to the carillon playing pretty classical pieces that I didn't recognize. I felt so relaxed and free with her.

I truly loved Nonni's independent, feisty spirit and her strength, even in the wake of her misfortunes. Maybe her life mirrored opera, I thought. This proved to be a source of strength and inspiration to me. I slowly came to realize that it wasn't my Mom's but a combination of Nonni Upstairs' and Nonni Next Door's *personalità* (personality) and *carattere* (character) that I would come to reflect.

There were also those occasions when we'd stroll, arm-in-arm, down Franklin Avenue to buy, then proceed to savor, freshly made, ricotta-filled cannoli from one of the bakeries that lined the bustling, commercialized street. I still loved being with Nonni Upstairs, although her bossy, insistent treatment of me—just to remind me that *she*, not *quel buco nero*, was my mother by proxy—was sometimes a source of consternation. So, too, were her interminable tirades about how the Riccucci's as well as Bruno and Mary stole from my parents and us. She couldn't let go of all this, yelling in Italian, "there were hundreds of thousands of dollars; you three kids should have gotten most of that money, not the trifle they gave you. You didn't even get $25,000 each!" I'd calmly say to her, *"e troppo tardi, Nonni; non si poi fare niente adesso,"* (just let it go, Nonni; there's nothing we could do about it now anyway). I was tired of hearing about money all the time. I didn't care about the money; to me, it was blood money, anyway. My mother and father were dead and money could never change this for me. Nonni would only get further enraged by my indifference, sending her further into an Italian, verbally expletive frenzy.

My grandmother seemed less angry about the crank calls she was getting; this, on the other hand, sent *me* into an Italian, verbally expletive frenzy. Nonni told me that at least once a week she received a phone call where the woman on the other end, speaking in a soft ghostly voice, would say "*So la Tosca*" (this is Tosca). She recognized my Aunt Mary's voice. She was tormenting Nonni, trying to make her go mad, thinking my Mom was calling her from the dead. Nonni would simply yell in the phone, "*SCHTOP-eh Siciliana*," (Stop you Sicilian), and slam the phone down. This sent me into a rage; I said to her in Italian, "This is so sick; why is she doing this? *How* could she do this? Let's call the cops on her." Nonni would calmly say, "*quel bucco nero* is very clever. That's what she expects; she would claim I'm crazy and try to put me away. Don't worry, she can't hurt me; just ignore it, and don't say anything to her, because she'll deny it and make your life even more miserable."

Somehow, my aunt found out about my visits to Nonni's. My grandmother was convinced that it was Angie Toscana, who lived across the street from my grandmother and was one of my aunt's best friends. Angie's husband, Joe was the "best man" at Aunt Mary and Uncle Bruno's wedding. It was Angie, my grandmother insisted. Many bitter battles were fought between Aunt Mary and me over my visits to Nonni's. I was becoming the "problem" child.

Rich, who will forever be Ricci to me, couldn't seem to handle the stress that inevitably ensued from such pandemonium. He would eventually have nothing to do with my grandmother and Johnny. He needed peace and safety. Ricci was still "a-fraidy cat."

I think it was Ricci's innate fear, combined with his strong need for stability, safety and belonging that led him to accept, unconditionally, my Aunt Mary and Uncle Bruno as surrogate parents. He needed the protection of a home and family. I was not in a position to offer these or anything else to him.

Ricci began to resent me for not following his lead, being in sync, as we had been all our lives. And he was angry with me for "talking back" as he saw it, to my aunt. But, as much as I loved Ricci, I could not accede to his demands. First of all I would never accept my Uncle Bruno, the pervert, as a parent. And my aunt was mean and malicious, and showed compassion only to those who she could control and manipulate. How could anyone trust her? I really disliked her and tried to stay out of her path as much as possible. To be sure, I must have been, from her perspective, very complicated, truculent, and sullen; in other words, a great big pain in her ass. I was pretty morose about the loss of my parents and she didn't like, couldn't handle sulking of any kind.

How did she expect me to behave? Happy and optimistic? How was I suppose to feel and act? Is it okay to be sad, or is this emotion reserved for adults only? One thing, however, seemed relatively clear: It was not acceptable to cry. Anytime my Aunt Mary caught me crying, she would ask rhetorically: "Do you realize how ugly you look when you cry?" I think it was around this time that I started referring to her as Cruella DeVille. It wasn't that she was ugly in terms of her looks, as was the character in one of favorite movies when I was a kid, *101 Dalmatians*. On the contrary, she was very attractive, especially in her youth. She had a deep olive, Mediterranean complexion, dark eyes and black wavy hair. I remember looking at the old photos of her—she was gorgeous, almost as much as Sophia Loren. But unfortunately, good looks do not always correlate with personality and temperament.

So, Ricci was beginning to pull away from me, his little sister. I blamed Mary for coming between us, because she was the adult; Ricci was very young and naïve. At 96 Hawley Street, Ricci was all I had left of my parents, our home, and the past. My aunt knew he was the only somebody that I really needed and loved, but she took him away from me. I felt another crack in my heart; as with opera, the scene had abruptly shifted and I was perpetually waiting for the other shoe to drop.

Act IV. Scene 1.
Signore, Ascolta

("*My God, Hear Me*," from Puccini's *Turandot*)

Starting 8th grade in midyear at a new school, Martin Kellogg, was a challenge. Because I had been in advanced courses at Vogel Junior High in Torrington, my new guidance counselor, without even evaluating my skill level, placed me in advanced courses. With the stroke of a pen, I found myself in courses for which I wasn't even remotely prepared. I was in an algebra class, midyear, yet I had never performed an algebraic equation before in my life. I was behind, and had a lot of catching up to do. I was developing a sick, queasy feeling in my stomach about school.

I had a hard time making friends, too. On my first day of school, Aunt Mary arranged for me to walk to school with some girls from the neighborhood. Ricci was in high school, so he walked with my cousin Little Johnny, whom we now called just John, and his friends. I walked to school with Sue DePaolis and a couple of other girls, but they didn't seem too happy to have "the new kid on the block" foisted upon them. Not very long afterwards, the wisecracks started about my unstylish hair and wardrobe, and my height—I was a tall 5'9" for a thirteen-year-old. I was boney, flat-chested, wore braces on my teeth, and unlike the other girls, didn't wear any makeup, because it never occurred to me to change my physical appearance. I put up with it, fighting them along the way, until I decided it would be less aggravating to walk alone. And so I did.

I pretty much kept to myself during this time, feeling out of place, out of step, and just plain anomalous. I don't think I ever felt so alone in all my life. Granted, I must have been, to say the least, a bit of an enigma to my classmates. And, some of those dick-heads like Doug Hope, Jimmy Grigas and Jimmy Coady (a.k.a. the nose picker and eater) didn't make it any easier. They made fun of my clothes and my general appearance. If I were still in Torrington, I would have confronted these jerks and called them a bunch of "shitheads." Instead, I felt ugly and worthless, and what self-esteem remained could fit in a pissant's eye. I no longer had the fire inside of me, the passion to fight.

I rode my bike all the time, even in the inclement weather. My cousin Nancy would tease me, telling me that in the winter she wouldn't be surprised to see me riding my bike with snow chains on my bicycle tires. My bike enabled me to get away from 96 Hawley Street and find some peace and solitude. I went for long rides or sometimes walked my bike up Newington Mountain, a scenic overlook of the town that had quiet, remote spots that no one seemed to know or care about. I would park my bike and sit for hours on a huge boulder protruding from the side of the mountain, watching the tiny people and soundless events going on in the town below me.

When I got hungry during the day, I'd stop at a grocery store and eat something. I'd park my bike outside, lock it, and walk through the grocery store with a shopping cart pretending to shop. Only, I'd be eating my lunch. I'd rip off a hunk of Italian bread from a bag, open a pack of salami lunchmeat and eat as I meandered up and down the isles with my cart, randomly plopping items into it to make it look as though I was shopping. I always ate a handful of Oreos or a couple of Hostess Chocolate Cupcakes for dessert. I think that because I wasn't physically removing anything from the store, I was able to rationalize to myself that I wasn't really stealing. Anyway, if I got caught, maybe I'd be sent to reform school, which had to be a step up from 96 Hawley. I never got caught, though, probably because I never hit the same grocery store twice in the same week.

I would leave the scantily filled shopping cart in an empty isle and make for the door. Only, I felt compelled—perhaps it was my conscience—to buy something. I usually bought a small carton of milk to wash down my meal. I wanted soda, but something in the back of my head told me to do the right thing and drink the milk.

I often rode my bike to the Newington library, about 3 miles from 96 Hawley, where I developed a camaraderie with the stillness, solitude and tranquility of reading. I would sit in the quietude and read for hours. I gradually learned to spend time alone and eventually welcomed the opportunity to do so; and I was growing intellectually. Even when people surrounded me, I felt a raw sense of aloneness. I begin to live mostly in my head.

For some inexplicable reason, I gravitated toward the "bleak, misanthropic section," as the librarian mockingly dubbed them when she directed me to the works of Schopenhauer, Nietzsche and Slyvia Plath. The writings of the two German philosophers were so dense and cryptic that it took me several attempts to discern their meaning. Through every iteration I gained some new insight, but in the end, I'm not sure I completely understood their ideas or scholarship. Yet, something drew me to Schopenhauer's pessimistic, anti-rationalistic, nihilistic tendencies. I came to admire his lack of respect for authority and his convictions about existence, or lack thereof: life is, because the world is, purposeless; existence consists of pain and boredom.

My interpretation of Schopenhauer went something like this: it's not so much the case that happiness is derived from misery but, rather that misery *sustains* life—the will to live stems from pain and suffering, not happiness, the latter of which is only an ephemeral illusion. As a corollary, we function more effectively as human beings when we are miserable and in pain. Or, maybe I was simply justifying my own existence at the time.

From my reading of Schopenhauer, the meaning of music to my life also seemed clearer. In *The World as Will and Representation*, he wrote, "When music suitable to any scene, action, event, or environment is played, it seems to disclose to us its most secret meaning." The meaning of opera to my life suddenly became more elucidated, even though I had stopped listening to it.

I was also fascinated and somewhat astounded by Schopenhauer's essay, "On Women." Intellect, he propounded, was a female characteristic, while the capacity for emotions was male. He believed that intellect was inherited from mothers, while will from fathers. At first blush, I was very impressed by his unorthodox views about the sexes. But on closer inspection—my fifth time reading it—Schopenhauer's ugly version of truth revealed itself: first, he did not recognize the possibility of female genius. Only men had the rare capacity to be geniuses. Second, according to Schopenhauer, will is primary, the true inner being, while the intellect is secondary, the accident of substance. Women are superficial and childlike while men are substantial and superior. Women, he concludes, will always be the weaker, substandard sex.

It wasn't that I could claim to be a feminist at the time, but his disparaging views of women so infuriated and affronted me. Most of the women in my life—my mother, Nonni Next Door, Nonni Upstairs—were strong, resolute, and self-assured. Schopenhauer's philosophy did not, by any stretch of the imagination, reflect my experiences. So, I decided to ditch his works and move on to something I thought might be lighter, namely Nietzsche, whose attacks on the hypocrisy of traditional European morality corresponded with my own sense of reality at the time. Corruption and decadence are pervasive, yet are rationalized away by the ideals of Judeo-Christianity. Those in power, namely the ecclesiastics, maintain their power by deceiving the masses through their delivery of hypocritical, specious teachings.

My spin on this was very simple: Here is my uncle, a paragon of morality in the community, loved and respected by all. The uttering of his name alone evoked the highest adulation, fawning, respect and deference. Yet, he had everyone fooled, even his own wife and children; he was the proverbial man behind the curtain. God knows who else has fallen prey to his brand of debauchery, bestiality, lecherousness and marauding. The meek and feeble are repressed and silenced. They have lost their voices. Our will to power is crushed and extinguished; we are disempowered. This Nietzsche guy, I thought, really has a grip on reality.

But then I unexpectedly came across a contemporary interpretation of Nietzsche's oeuvre: philosophical support for the Nazi's annihilation of millions of Jews during World War II. I'm not certain if it was the Italian-Catholic guilt thing going on (*mia colpa*, as I learned it), or a sense of astonishment and indignation, but it was around this time that I developed a lifelong obsession with the Holocaust and the Third Reich. First, I wondered why I hadn't learned about these atrocities in my formal schooling. Was I the product of a whitewashed, anesthetized, bourgeois, "white" education? Suburbia often propagates insularism, but how was it that such a singular, consequential event in history escaped the attention of my educators?

And, I wondered, how does such a crime against humanity befall a civilized society? Who *allows* it to occur? What brand of hatred, or more, indifference can so infect humankind that an entire people can be exterminated without challenge or formulated intervention?

I wasn't certain if my polemics around the fascists and Nazis were naive, or if my own ignorance had stirred such a passion in me that I craved the truth. In any case, Nietzsche was the provocateur.

As with Schopenhauer, I felt a deep sense of betrayal. I knew that I could no longer seek meaning and edification from this German philosopher, so, I abandoned my efforts to digest Nietzsche.

I moved on to Sylvia Plath and *The Bell Jar*. What attracted me to Plath was her sadness and hopeless despair;

this was very evident in her poetry but strikingly so in *The Bell Jar*. In this novel, Plath tries to make sense of her turbulent life through the autobiographical fictitious character Esther Greenwood, whose mental breakdown leads to madness, a suicide attempt, shock treatment (why not a lobotomy, I wondered?), and then cure. Sylvia Plath's life parallels Esther's up through the point of cure—Plath successfully killed herself in 1963, one month after *The Bell Jar* was first released in England.

I was also drawn to *The Bell Jar* and Plath because through all of her pain and anguish, she still was able to leaven her sadness with humor. One passage has always stuck with me. When the character Buddy Willard decides to show Esther, his girlfriend, what a naked man looks like, Plath writes: "He just stood there in front of me and I kept on staring at him. The only thing I could think of was turkey neck and turkey gizzards and I felt very depressed."

After having read *The Bell Jar* as well as Schopenhauer and Nietzsche I came to know something that I suppose I had known for a long time: that there are two paths in life—survival which is what Esther Greenwood chooses, or the afterlife, seeking peace in death, that which Sylvia Plath, Bellini's *Norma*, and my Dad chose.

I never checked any books out of the library, because it was nobody's business first, that I spent time at the library and second, what I was reading. If Aunt Mary and Uncle Bruno found out, they would tease and ridicule me unmercifully because they believed that education and higher learning were strictly in the domain of men. When I started high school, they informed me that I would be taking the "business course route" (bookkeeping, typing, office machines) and not the pre-college courses, since I wouldn't be going to college. They must have contacted my high school guidance counselor, Miss Main, who also steered me into the business track.

"But I want to go to college," I said. "My parents wanted me and my brothers to go to college; they saved for it."

Mary simply said, "We're not sending you to college. It's a waste of money, since you'll just get married after high school and have kids; you won't need a career. Look at Claudia; it's what she did. And Nancy is engaged." That parturition could be the raison d'être for women so incensed me I thought my head would explode!

But, there was no point in arguing. Nor was it worth it for me to tell them that I hardly viewed Claudia as a role model. Claudia was very beautiful and street-smart, but like her mother, was a bit zany. Nonni at some point had cleverly dubbed her, "*la monaca allegra*" (the merry, happy-go-lucky nun). Despite the vicissitudes of her life, Nonni maintained her sharp wit and wry sense of humor.

Just before getting married, Claudia thought she had a calling to be a Catholic nun. She must have been inspired by the movie, "Song of Bernadette," because that was the name she took. Catholic nuns were required to adopt a new name, one of a saint they wished to emulate. But Claudia was nothing like the movie-version of Bernadette, who was a young asthmatic French girl from the 19th century who had visions of the Virgin Mary in a grotto in Lourdes. St. Bernadette was a peasant girl, very humble, unadulterated, unassuming and just plain simple. Claudia, the day before she entered the convent, was on the Connecticut shore wearing a slinky bikini with half her body parts exposed. She was making-out on a beach towel with her boyfriend, Gregg. Anyway, she lasted about a week in the convent, or nunnery as I called it; what she must have romanticized the life of a noviciate to be became a nightmare to her: scrubbing floors on her hands and knees and abstaining from just about everything good in life. Shortly after her departure, she got married to Danny, the divorced one. As much as I loved Claudia and her nutty ways, I couldn't help but rhetorically ask myself "This could be a role model?!"

My aunt and uncle's way of thinking was the complete antithesis to everything my parents had taught me. My parents had a strong desire for their children to get a college education, since neither they nor their parents had the opportunity to do so. A very high premium was placed on education by my parents and grandparents; this was only one of the many values discounted and devalued my Aunt Mary and Uncle Bruno.

It was toward the end of the school year at Martin Kellogg when a girl named Nancy Jutras from my algebra class asked me to join her and her friends, Vicky Zuraw, Sue Condren and JoAnn Yannas, at a Friday night dance. She was about the kindest person I had met at school and one of the few who was willing to strike up a conversation with me. The dance was from 7 to 10:30 p.m. at Martin Kellogg's gymnasium and did I want to join them? Sure, I had said.

My cousin Nancy drove me to the school that Friday evening in her cool, green VW bug. When we pulled up to the front door, however, something seemed wrong. Older couples were walking into the gym; and they were wearing flashy, flairy country-western duds. When I rolled down the window to ask what was going on in the gym, a woman replied, "square dancing." My stomach dropped.

Why would Nancy Jutras fool me like this? Was she like everyone else just finding clever ways to ridicule me? My cousin Nancy said she was sorry and drove me back to the house. I was too embarrassed to say anything.

When we arrived back at 96 Hawley Street, everyone commented underneath their sneers and smirks about how Nancy Jutras made a real fool of me, and what a rotten thing to do. Well, no sooner had I walked in, than the phone rang; it was Nancy. She had just returned, too, from the gym, and found out that there was square dancing that particular Friday evening; how sorry she was that she had made the mistake. We talked for about a half-an-hour on the phone, my longest phone call ever. Afterwards, everyone said it was about time I had made some girlfriends and spent time yakking on the phone with them. Nancy and I began a lifelong friendship that evening.

Act IV. Scene 2.
Nessun Dorma
("No One Sleeps," from Puccini's *Turandot*)

There is nothing indecent about the human anatomy. And, because of my unbridled upbringing, the body just was. It was nothing to fear and there wasn't anything mysterious about it. It was merely a functional rudiment of life. No big deal!

So, why did my uncle exposing himself to me paralyze me with such fear and anguish? I remember talking on the telephone and there he'd be, standing off in a dark corner holding his wanker in his hand and wiggling it at me. Part of me would think, "You'd better stick that pathetic, shriveled up old thing—'turkey neck and turkey gizzards'—back in your pants before I whack it off." But, he wasn't being funny. This pervert wanted me to look at him so he could get his rocks off.

Don't look. Ignore him. There's nothing to be afraid of. All the while, tears were streaming down my face. I am so frightened, ashamed and powerless. I am also confused. What makes him think he can get away with this, when other people are in the house? But he must not care, and he *does* get away with it. I was talking with my friend Nancy on the phone who asked, "Are you okay?" I said, "I think I'm getting a cold."

I didn't know why this was happening. What had I done to bring this on? Maybe it had something to do with that time when I was five or six years old and my mother caught me playing with myself, masturbating was the word I later learned. She hadn't reprimanded me, but maybe my mother told her brother Bruno about it and this was the reason for what was happening to me.

Maybe it was that time when I was about nine years old, exploring the neighborhood around my Dad's shoe store and that strange guy who was waxing his 1964 1/2 pale yellow, four-on-the-floor Mustang convertible with black leather bucket seats called me over to look at his car. I went, of course, because Mustangs were one of my favorite cars. He told me I could sit in the driver's side, bucket seat, if I cupped his *pistilino* in my hand. I started to reach for it because I didn't understand the significance of such an act; it just seemed stupid and pointless to me. Then, for some unknown reason I began to cry and ran back to my father's store. I told my Dad what had happened and for the second time in his life, he locked up his store in the middle of the afternoon. He asked me to take him to where this guy was which I did. My Dad was so outraged I thought he was going to beat the crap out of this psychotic degenerate. My Dad ended his verbal tirade by telling him he needed help because he was sick, and that he would come around in a few days to make sure that he went and found help. After that, I never saw that yellow Mustang in the neighborhood again. Anyway, maybe it was this incident, which accounted for what my uncle was now doing to me, for I was at a complete loss for an explanation.

I made it a point to never be alone with him in a room, car, or even the backyard. Once when I was in the basement getting clothes out of the dryer, I heard him lumbering down the stairs. He was fat, out of shape and always out of breath; he was a heavy smoker and drank a few glasses of scotch on the rocks every night, followed by several glasses of wine with his meal. He sat at the head of the dining room table and commanded everyone as though we were his slaves—get me this, or get me that. And, if his bottle of wine wasn't next to his place setting when he sat down, he'd slammed his fist down hard on the table and bellow, "Where is my wine? Why isn't here?" He'd tap his big fat index finger on the table where the wine bottle should have been and demand, "That bottle should be here when I sit down." Even when Bruno was not in motion, sitting in a chair, he breathed heavily. That wheezing made me shudder.

I continued to pull towels and sheets out of the dryer as I watched him from the corner of my eye. "What had he told Mary his reason was for being in the basement?" I wondered. As he came up behind me, I threw a towel at him and bolted for the stairs. He grabbed the back of my shirt, but I managed to tug away from him without ripping my shirt. I could hear him laughing as I ran up the stairs.

Sometimes I just couldn't get away. And, he was bigger and stronger than I. My mouth would open to scream, but no words or sounds came out. I had no voice. I was silenced by my own inexorable fear, which made me both angry and ashamed. I would effortlessly step out of my body; I would float upwards, towards the ceiling and look down on what was happening. I saw myself standing there, but it wasn't me; it was a pathetic shell of a human, whose eyes were shut so tight that her face was contorted and ugly. Teardrops moistened her cheeks.

I sought refuge in my fail-safe: expletives. I would yell down to that shivering, pitiful thing, "Hey you stupid shithead. Stop him. Don't let him touch you like that. What the fuck's the matter with you, you dumb shitass?

As I had learned, just after my mother died, cursing was effective, cathartic. And so it continued to serve me well, although it did sometimes completely besiege me; like that incident at the one and only drug store in the center of Newington, when I was buying a bottle of shampoo. I started sniffing the vast array of bottles for the least offensive scent. In the process, one of the bottles slipped out of my hands and crashed down hard onto the floor. There was shampoo everywhere, including all over my jeans. I wasn't even cognizant that someone else was in the aisle before this diarrheal explosion of expletives flushed out of my mouth. When I realized someone was not too far from me in the same aisle, I slowly turned to the person, made eye contact with her, smiled politely and said, "Tourette's Syndrome." I then proceeded to walk slowly out of the store, phlegmatically telling the cashier on my way out that some ninny had spilled a bottle of shampoo in aisle four.

My uncle, who I obliquely began referring to as the Marquis de Sade, took something very fundamental from me through all of this: he took my free-spiritedness, my innocence, my sense of safety and innate trust for humankind, my sense of well-being. And, this spectacle, this waste of human skin was actually my mother's brother. What would my Mom think of such unspeakable behavior? Did he even care? If my Dad were here, he'd beat the shit out of this perverse, demented, sociopath. I wish he were here.

I don't think I slept soundly the entire five years I lived at my aunt and uncle's. Not only did I live in fear of potential attacks at night from the Marquis, but I regularly had nightmares that scared me to the point where once I awoke, I was afraid to go back to sleep. Aside from the nightmares about my Dad's death, I had recurring nightmares of being maimed and mutilated, or of being chased through dark underground tunnels by something I could never quite discern, but instinctively knew to fear. I often woke from these nightmares screaming.

Other times, I dreamt of my parents, all of us together again, a happy, safe family. I was glad for these dreams, but also saddened, because even in this state of suspended consciousness, there is a vague notion of delusive reality. I see my parents and feel the joy of being with them again after their long absence. But, in my dream, how is it that I know they have been gone, and where exactly have they been? Why do I have this haunting impulse that they are merely an illusion, part of an apocryphal fantasy?

Sometimes I think I see my mother or father standing at the foot of my bed, trying desperately to pull me towards them. These dreams, too, so disturb me because I awake to find that I am still here in this bed at 96 Hawley Street, and that I cannot leave with my parents.

Nonni was now gone, and although I shared a bedroom with my cousin Nancy, she was often out in the evenings with friends or her fiancé, Artie. I soon discovered at least one functional method for ensuring some safekeeping during these seemingly endless nights: I would lie on the floor of the bedroom, with my body pressed up tightly against the bedroom door. In the event I would fall asleep before my cousin returned home, it served as a barricade to prevent my uncle from entering the room. (Why didn't these old houses have any locks on the doors?!) If my uncle attempted to push the door in, I would wake up and could scream. For hours, I would lie awake, peering out of the thin crack at the bottom of the door, praying not to see footsteps approaching. I repeated "Hail Mary's," over and over again in my head. I was still pissed off at God for having taken my Mom, so I instead prayed to his mother. I had learned a lot from opera and one thing was to pray when you are in trouble, even if it doesn't help. If I did see Bruno's footsteps coming toward the door, I would scream in order to scare him away; others in the house would just attribute the screams to another one of my nightmares. It proved to be an effective deterrent. On the occasions my cousin planned to sleep at one of her friends, I barely slept at all. I would wake up in the morning from an unsound, troubled sleep with my face still pressed closely up against the bedroom door, drooling.

Once, when I knew my cousin would be out late, and I just wanted, needed to sleep in my bed, I barricaded the door shut with a chair, thinking I would wake up once my cousin tried to get in. Apparently, I felt so secure with that chair up against the door, I went into such a deep sleep that I never heard my cousin struggling and pushing her way into the room. The next morning I was sitting at the kitchen table drinking my coffee. My aunt and uncle were getting ready for work, but they as well as the entire household could hear Nancy when she came downstairs, belligerently reaming me out for barricading the door.

"Are you crazy or something?" She screamed at me. "Don't you ever do anything so stupid and inconsiderate like that again."

My uncle knew better than to say anything and my aunt just dismissed it as another instance of Norma going off the deep end. I just sat there quietly, with my head lowered over my hot cup of coffee.

ACT IV. SCENE 3.
UNA FURTIVA LAGRIMA

("*A Secret Tear*," from Donizetti's
L'elisir D'amore)

I started my freshman year of high school in the fall of 1970. Nonni was gone. I felt as if I was going deeper and deeper into a hole. My biggest fear was keeping my uncle off me. I can't tell anyone; I keep it a secret for fear I will not be believed. I'm afraid to even tell my friends even though they have become the most important facet of my life. I'm afraid they will think that I am crazy; I wished I could trust them but I feel so betrayed by the actions of what I thought was my *family*—my aunts and uncles—that I say nothing. I was too fearful, waiting for that other shoe to drop.

Still I didn't feel quite alone when I was with my friends. They were my support system and in a way, my surrogate family since I was getting nothing resembling familial care and support from anybody at 96 Hawley Street.

I had developed a few friendships, but Nancy Jutras, Cheryl Litwin and Karen St. John were my best friends. They were so different from one another, but each would come to reflect certain of my own characteristics. Karen, for example, was very spiritual, soulful, earthy, and funky. I met her walking home from school one day. She lived about 8 blocks away from 96 Hawley Street and we seemed to click, so we started walking to and from high school together. It was a welcome relief from walking alone every day. She was a bit quiet and shy and she didn't judge people. She accepted me even though I still looked like a geek. I knew from the outset, she was a kindred spirit.

Karen was very thin, and at 5' 2" I towered over her; by the time I was fourteen, I reached 5'9 1/2" and was one of the tallest girls in school. She had long brown wavy hair that naturally draped over her face, which had a very wholesome, natural clean look. One would never guess she wore makeup. I liked this, since I hadn't yet started to wear makeup. I also liked that she wore bell-bottomed jeans a lot, even to school. I thought this was really cool. And she typically wore a white or beige flowing, gauzy-linen bell-sleeved blouse. She could have been a "flower child" if, like me, she weren't a bit on the square side. Unlike the hippies in our school, we didn't drink or smoke pot, for the time being anyway.

After walking home from school we would sit on her front stoop or mine and just hang out, watching the cars go by, getting to know each other better. Karen was an only child and her parents were overly protective of her. She couldn't stay out past nine and she had to spend Sundays with them going to flea markets and antique shows. Mr. and Mrs. St. John were Civil War buffs and had an almost obsessive collection of paraphernalia cluttered about their very tiny, cottage-style home, where their obesely fat, one-eyed cat Zippo darted about like a frenetic squirrel caught in the middle of rush-hour traffic. I would occasionally join them and liked perusing Civil War memorabilia particularly the little scraps of paper supposedly signed by President Lincoln, the tarnished canteens, and the small antique photo frames with faded black and white pictures of young Union soldiers in their disheveled uniforms, holding muskets with their "deer-in-the-headlight" eyes staring back at the camera. Mr. St. John had a sporty, blue Dodge Charger and his driving reminded me of my grandfather's. He drove at excessively fast speeds, which didn't seem to bother Mrs. St. John or Karen. I loved it, and dared him to pass as many cars as possible. It felt like I was in the kid's seat of Nonno and Nonni Next Door's dark-blue, hardtop 1957 Cadillac Eldorado Seville.

One of Karen's and my favorite things to do was climb the under-explored Newington Mountain, where I had visited many times by myself. She was the only person I wanted to share this experience with because her inner peace mirrored the quietude of this remote, abandoned spot. We'd meander up the sparsely wooded dirt path just off the end of Hawley Street to the top, which was marked by densely packed varieties of pine trees. We'd sit for hours on the flat surface of the boulder, sometimes without even exchanging a word, as we looked down at the town with its tiny busy people and cars going somewhere or nowhere very fast.

My friendship with Nancy Jutras blossomed in high school. Nancy was about 5'8", very slender with long dirty-blond hair. I liked that we were about the same height; I didn't feel so gawky around her. Nancy squinted a lot because she needed glasses but refused to wear them because only nerds wore eyeglasses. I was always envious of her small hips and flat chest. As I was getting older, my hips and boobs were getting overly robust, and I hated this. It was then that I started to develop poor posture, slightly hunching my shoulders over so as to de-emphasize my boobs. My cousin Nancy would say, "Norma, you look great; you're becoming a woman!" I'd say, "Is it really necessary for women who want to look good to have these flaccid appendages?"

Nancy Jutras lived in a huge house on Main Street, about 4 miles from 96 Hawley Street. Nancy was one of seven brothers and sisters and she once told me that, of all her friends I was her parent's favorite. This made me feel special, because I was very fond of them. They were old world Italian, and so kind to me, despite the fact they were always screaming at their kids, especially Mrs. Jutras. Nancy would scream right back at her, which amazed me. I never spoke to my parents or grandparents that way, nor would I have ever dared to speak to Mary or Bruno in that fashion. I'd be slapped in the face or head! What astonished me was that one minute they would be engaged in a virulent verbal exchange—"Get the hell out of my kitchen," Mrs. Jutras would bark at Nancy, who responded, "Jeeze-is, would you get off my, back?" Nancy never said, "Jesus" or "Christ;" just "Jeeze-is" or "Chripe" so as not to step over the line with her Mom. But then in the next minute, they'd have a civil exchange as though the screaming match had not transpired:

Nancy: "What's for dinner tonight, Mom?"

Mrs. Jutras: "Meatloaf; ask Norma if she wants to stay for dinner."

The Friday-night sleepovers at Nancy Jutras' were a particularly welcomed respite from 96 Hawley. I was able to sleep soundly without having to worry about Bruno's attempts to corner me. After swimming in the Jutras' huge above-ground pool or just hanging out in the backyard of Vicky's, Sue's or JoAnn's—who all called me "cooch,"—we'd head to Nancy's house by around 10 p.m. Everyone in the house would be asleep by then, so Nancy and I would quietly open up the large sofa-bed in the living room, and watch the gaudy, yet entertaining Elvira, who hosted the Friday-night, double-feature horror show with B-rated movies. She looked like a tawdry tramp, in her black attire, heavily applied black eye makeup and long straight black hair. She wore dark red lipstick and too much bright red blush. And her accentuated milky white boobs were pushed up so high she could almost touch them with her chin. Mostly, though, Nancy and I talked, laughed, gossiped and prattled on about movies, teachers or just idle nonsense. I particularly liked to tell her some of the corny new jokes I learned from my cousin John, like:

Me: "Did you ever smell mothballs?"

Nancy: "Yeah, of course."

Me: "Oh, how did ever you get his tiny, little legs apart?"

Or, Me: A woman goes into a supermarket and asks the grocer, "Sir, to you have any nuts?"

The grocer says, "No ma'am."

The woman then asks, "What about dates, do you have any dates?"

The grocer wryly responds, "Lady, if I had any nuts, I'd have dates."

Nancy would sometimes tell me about her boyfriend, Steve Miner, whom she would eventually marry. Nancy was more interested in boys than I was, but I patiently listened as she talked. Once I asked her about Steve's father, who's right side of his face was severely disfigured. I regretted having asked. Nancy told me very diffidently that when Steve's mother left his father, he took a gun and shot himself in the face. She pitied him, and was clearly embarrassed to tell me about the incident. It made me cringe when she told me, and I wondered why he didn't die, like my Dad had from his gunshot wound. I had never spoken to my friends about my Dad's death. It wasn't that I was ashamed of what he had done, but rather I sought to protect him, because there is mystique around suicide that few understand. The general view is that someone who attempts or successfully commits suicide is batty and belongs in the loony bin. No one really stops to think about the circumstances surrounding why one would whack themselves off. Nancy's hesitancy in telling me the story bore out my beliefs. So, whenever someone asked me: "How did your parents die?" I responded, "My Mom died of cancer and my Dad died of a broken heart."

At around midnight, Nancy and I would sneak down to the huge freezer Mrs. Jutras kept—well stocked I might add—in the basement. We each selected a frozen T.V. dinner—turkey with stuffing was my favorite, which somehow tasted infinitely better than those my father, brothers and I ate after my Mom died. We'd get them steaming hot, and then proceeded to gobble them up in front of the television. Sometime around two or three in the morning, we'd fall asleep with the T.V., now snowy white from being off the air, humming in the background.

There was one night when we were in the downstairs bathroom washing up, getting ready for our Friday night movies, and Nancy was standing in the medicine cabinet mirror swabbing a dampened cotton ball across her forehead. I suddenly smelled something very familiar. I breathed in very deeply and froze. Nancy was looking at my reflection in the mirror and said, "What is it?" I picked up the clear glass apothecary bottle on top of the toilet tank; it had clear liquid inside, and the bottle read "Humphrey's Witch Hazel." It smelled like my mother the last time I saw her in the hospital. I never realized that smells could be recalled so vividly. I got tears in my eyes when I took a big whiff out of the bottle, and Nancy said, "Are you crying?" I said, "No, the smell of this stuff is so strong it's making my eyes water." The next day, I walked to Newington Drug Store in the center of town and bought the largest bottle, albeit plastic, of witch hazel I could find.

I met Cheryl Litwin in Mrs. Dath's "Office Skills" class when I was a sophomore. I didn't know it then, but Cheryl would remain one of the most faithful of friends throughout my life. Cheryl was short like Karen, but she had long straight corn-blonde hair that always looked silky smooth. She had beautiful blue eyes and an infectious laugh. She was also on the rubenesque side, and was strikingly attractive.

I was a bad influence on Cheryl, but I liked to think in a good way. Her first experience with liquor, for example, was when I got her sauced. I started drinking more and more in my sophomore year in high school. I mostly drank beer but would eventually move on to what I classified as the "hard" stuff: peach or blackberry brandy. It was my beverage of choice even though, on the first few gulps from the bottle, it always burned going down my throat. But as I slowly discovered, it was effective for self-induced alcoholic stupors, which helped me escape the revulsion of living at 96 Hawley Street.

One day, Cheryl and I were hanging out with Ricci and my cousin John at 96 Hawley. Ricci had become very aloof with me, but he tolerated me when my friends were around. I asked, "Who's ready for a cocktail?" When Cheryl said, "I've never had alcohol," I raised my eyebrows, smirked at Ricci and John and said, "I'll fix 'em." I filled up a tumbler three-quarters of the way with Bacardi Rum from my uncle's liquor cabinet, added a splash of Coke and several cubes of ice. Actually, my uncle referred to the cabinet as a "dry bar." My uncle tried hard to fit in with the white, bourgeois business community in Newington. He even played golf. But, try as he did, he still looked like one of those greasy, fat Italian men in *The Godfather*. When Cheryl, myself and another friend went to the drive-in movie during a mild snow storm to see *The Godfather* when it premiered in 1972, I thought to myself, when I saw the character Clemenza roly-polying across the screen, "hey, there's Bruno!"

I gave the drink to Cheryl, and said, "Don't drink it all at once." She gulped it down, and the next thing I see is Cheryl wandering around the floor, on her hands and knees, pretending to be a dog. She was drunk. Ricci and

John were egging her on, and I was laughing so hard, I barely made it to the bathroom.

Then there was the time I taught Cheryl how to play strip ghost. Ghost is a game where you sit in a circle and someone starts to build a word by offering a single letter. Each subsequent person adds another letter, trying to avoid forming a word. If a person forms a word, she or he gets a "G." The first person to get all the letters to spell out "ghost" loses. My twist to this game was anytime you form a word on your turn, you not only get a letter, but you have to remove an article of clothing. Only before we started playing, I went up to my room and secretly put on every piece of jewelry I could think of without being too obvious. This would assure that I would never need to remove an article of clothing. As a fail-safe, I also slipped into my bathing suit, a bikini. In any event, there was no way I planned on shedding any clothing, since Ricci and John would be present. So too was Ricci's best friend, Billy DeMila, who I had a wild crush on, but don't think he ever knew or cared. Billy was kind, gentle, funny and innocuous. But, I was still not interested in boys in that way.

So, we proceeded to play strip ghost. In each successive round, Cheryl found herself losing and shedding first earrings, then a watch, and next would be either her jeans or blouse. The round started with John offering a "b." I added an "o." Everyone's eyes were glued to Cheryl, who was next, and clearly racking her brain for a letter, so as not to form a word. After a brief pause, she thought she had it; she blurted out, in a victorious tone—thinking, we learned later, of the word boat—the letter "a!" We all screamed "boa," and laughed as we prodded her to remove either her jeans or her blouse. After much coaxing, she slowly started to pull her pants down when suddenly we hear someone's key turning in the lock at the front door. Without time to even look at one another, we all dispersed, with Cheryl trying to run upstairs, her jeans still hanging down around her ankles. We were laughing so hard, we barely heard my cousin Nancy walking in, yelling, into the ostensibly vacant house, "Anyone home?"

Cheryl and I sat next to each other in the last row of Mrs. Dath's class. Cheryl had a good sense of humor and I could always make her laugh with my vast repertoire of antics. I was forever telling her bad jokes especially about the pedantry of the class (learning how to file—I mean, really!), trying to grab her homework off her desk or sneaking a peek at her test answers only to hear Mrs. Dath yelling in her whinny, high-pitched voice to the back of the room, "Norma, will you *please* leave Cheryl alone?" or "Norma, will you stop pestering Cheryl." Cheryl and I would furtively glance at one another, lower our heads, and try to contain our inexhaustible laughter.

I often shrouded my jokes to Cheryl in reality, which made them even funnier to her and me. Like this: "So, Cheryl, my cousin John went party hopping Saturday night, and he said there was this one house that had a huge, brass toilet bowl. But, because he left the party so drunk, by Sunday morning he couldn't remember where the house was. So, he went from house to house Sunday afternoon, knocking on people's doors, asking, 'Did you have a party last night and do you have a big brass toilet bowl?' Everyone just looked at him oddly, kept saying no and slammed the door in his face. Then, he went to this one house and a woman answered the door, and he again asked, 'Did you have a party last night and do you have a big brass toilet bowl?' And the woman stepped back from the front door, and yelled into the house, 'Harry, here's the guy who shit in your tuba.'"

I will think back on these as the very best of times, where I was still young enough to feel blithely uninhibited with someone who, in retrospect, would truly and inimitably be one of my very best of friends. It is a moment in time that would forever be frozen in my cavernous vacuum of recollections.

My cousin Nancy was six years older than me and not around most of the time, but she treated me like a sister and made me feel safe. She would often say, "You're like my baby sister," and I began to refer to her as my sister. One time Nancy overhead her mother threatening to put me in an orphanage, and she ran to me, hugged me and said, "I'd never let that happen, Norma. I'd take you before she could ever do that." When I then ran upstairs crying, I could hear Nancy screaming at Mary for scaring and bullying me.

Nancy had a good bookkeeping job at the Grand Union grocery store in Glastonbury, drove a cool green VW Bug, and was engaged to be married. She was high-spirited and zany; she reminded me of Lucy Ricardo from "I Love Lucy," because she was always doing nutty things. Like that one time her friend Suzanne and I were riding home from a softball game in her bug. The music was blasting and as Aretha Franklin sang "Respect" we were all screaming the words and swaying and twisting our bodies to the rhythm. We were unaware of how fast Nancy was driving until a Newington police officer pulled us over. I looked out the rear window and yelled, "Oh, no, the pigs are after us." Nancy said, "Let me handle this; I know some of these guys, and they're pretty cool." When the officer approached the car, Nancy jumped out and said, "I'm so sorry, officer; the music was blaring and we were trying to dance so I didn't know I was speeding." Then, she poked her head in the car and said "come on Suzanne and Norm, let's show him." I jumped out of the backseat of the car and while Aretha was still singing, started bee-bopping with Nancy to the beat; Suzanne was doing the Pony by herself. The cop just looked at us with a smirk on his face; he shook his head and said, "Go home, lady. And don't quit your day job." We laughed, piled back in the car and drove away still jukin' to the music.

Nancy taught me a lot of ways to improve my external image and physical appearance, and God knows I needed it. She taught me how to set my hair, which was about waist-long, with those huge, juice-can-type rollers; how to apply facial make-up; what type of clothes were too queer to wear, and most importantly, how to use tampons. Oh happy days—no more yucky, stinky sanitary napkins, which really weren't all that sanitary. Oh, now I know where the vagina is!

By the time I was a junior, I looked pretty okay and actually felt good about my outer self. I only wore blue jeans to school, funky shirts and shoes, and often wore my hair in a single, thick braid, which draped down my back. Was I becoming a hippie? I had grown into my body, as disgusted as I was with it.

*On our way to Claudia's wedding. Note the nerdy
bow Nonni Upstairs FORCED me to wear.*

Cheryl (right) and I chilling on our way to Sound View Beach

Karen (left) and I on our way up Newington Mountain

Vicky Zuraw, Nancy Jutras and I (left to right)

Cousin John with his dog, Tammy

High school graduation

We seem to have this concentric circle of friends when we are in high school. There is the inner, primary circle, of which some will remain lifelong friends, like Nancy and Cheryl. And we will never know friendships like this again. Then there are the secondary and tertiary circles, friends that we sometimes misguidedly call our best friends, because this is what we do when we are in high school. In these circles, I have many friends. Some are very racy and some are what my Aunt Mary called "those antiwar hippies."

"I don't want those antiwar hippies coming around here," she would belch at me.

It's not that my friends did any war protesting to speak of; they merely wore faded, often torn tee shirts that read "**OUT OF VIETNAM**" or "**4 DEAD IN OHIO**." Subtle, but a statement it certainly made. My "hippie" friends, like Bobby and Maureen, liked to get high on pot, which was the generally preferred intoxicant of friends in my outer circles. They gave me a hard time because I wouldn't smoke with them. It isn't because I was opposed to it on grounds that it was illegal (or immoral and debased, as our teachers told us), but because I hated the smell and taste of it. It literally made me nauseous. Bobby, stoned out of his mind, would say, "Come on, Norma; take a hit. It won't hurt you." I'd invariably snap back at him, "Bobby, leave me the fuck alone; you know I hate the smell and taste of that shit."

I instead preferred my "booze," as I called it: peach or blackberry brandy. I was drinking a lot in those days. It got me through the days and nights and helped to further numb my already dull senses. My lack of sobriety in the early 1970s was probably a blessing for any number of reasons. For one thing, I somnambulated my way through that ass-wipe megalomaniac Nixon's Presidency, Watergate, and, despite the antiwar slogans on my friends' tee shirts, the horrors of the Vietnam War. The closest I got to protesting the country's involvement in Vietnam was my love for music: in this case, the Rolling Stones' "Gimme Shelter," Marvin Gaye's "What's Going On," and Edwin Starr's "War."

In another circle, I have some very promiscuous friends. Well, I don't think any of my friends were "doing it" as we called it back then—screwing or balling were the ugly terms the boys used. But, they were going beyond making out, to first and second bases, and some *may* have been going to third base, giving their boyfriends blowjobs. But I don't think so, because they surely would have told it. Just like Leanne, who once told me her boyfriend fingered her. I made a face and said "Fingered?" not knowing what that meant. And she said, "Yeah, you know, finger fucked." Pretending I knew what it was, I bluffed my way through, making something up: "Oh yeah, you mean, "ff'd." I didn't want to let on how naive I was. And despite the circumstances with the pig man, Bruno, I really was pretty clueless.

I was about fifteen when I found out how babies were made. I was at the beach with my Aunt Mary, and she asked why I wasn't in the water with Ricci and John. I said I had my period and bad cramps. And then she launched into it.

"Do you know why we get our periods?"

I replied, "I don't know and I don't care; I just hate it!"

Then she said, "It's for having babies. Do you know how babies are born?"

I replied, "Babies come from the stomach."

She asked, "Well, how do they get there?"

I pretended not to hear her, laid back down on my beach towel and turned up my small blue AM/FM transistor radio playing Diana Ross and The Supremes' "Reflections."

She continued loudly, "At night in bed, the man puts his penis in the woman's vagina. The vagina is where the period blood comes from."

And, then, trying to be smart, I sat up and said, "Yeah, well what if the woman is sleeping or has her pajamas on?"

My aunt started to laugh and said, "You wouldn't be sleeping through it, and you'd be in bed without clothes."

Yuk, I thought, and got up from my towel, and made my way down to the water's edge.

There was this one mentally challenged student in my class who had a lasting impression on me. Her name was Debbie; she was short, overweight, had stringy brown hair and pasty white skin. But, she was always smiling. I would wonder, "What's going on in her head?" The dumb-asses, Doug and the two Jimmy's would make fun of her calling her a "RE-tard." I would yell out at them, "You'll find the real RE-tards in the mirror, you stupid fuck heads." At which point they would say in unison, "ooooo" because I used the "f" word. Then they'd laugh and walk away. One day, Debbie was wearing this huge blue crystal topaz ring on her forefinger. It was very striking. I walked up to her and said, "Debbie; that's a beautiful ring; where'd you get it?" She said, "At the airport." And then she launched into this long litany about how she was directing air traffic at Bradley International Airport in Hartford. She held the back side of her hand up in the air, conspicuously displaying her ring, slightly twisting her wrist back and forth in hopes the light would refract from the intricate angles of the blue crystal, and made a short, staccatoed whistle sound as if she were directing an airplane into its gate. I envied her. I wished I could have her sense of innocence and oblivion to the world around me.

There weren't many black students in my high school class. Newington was a white suburb of Hartford and at the time had virtually no blacks or Hispanics. They were generally bused in from nearby cities that had large black populations like the small city of New Britain or the large inner city of Hartford. I liked the diversity of people in Hartford. But, my uncle hated it. He was a racist and sexist. He hated in his words, "niggers," "spics," "chinks," "sluts," and anyone else that wasn't "clean-cut," male, white, and of European heritage. I would seethe when he would use such language, and question how he could be so cruel, ignorant and unaccepting. Of course, if I had the courage, I would have shared a bit of what was on my mind: "Who the fuck do you think you are to judge other people, you sick, fat, shit-ass child molester? Don't you know you are the lowest form of all humanity? How dare you talk like this in my presence, you piece-of-shit bastard!"

I inherited the foul mouth from my maternal grandmothers. But, from no one in my past, was I ever exposed to such bigotry. I had never heard my parents or grandparents utter a single derogatory remark about blacks or any other racial or ethnic group. It was only the Sicilians that at least my grandparents made pejorative comments about, but not in the presence of my parents, who tolerated NO form of ethnic or class discrimination. For my grandparents it was almost instinctual.

I had a small crush on this short, cute guy named Vinnie. He had stunning immense, dark penetrating eyes. His short, black glistening afro accentuated his razor-bumped dark skin. He wore a shortly cropped goatee and his face was perfectly framed by eyeglasses like those worn by Malcolm X. He often wore a faded brown tee shirt that said in big bold black letters, "Imported from Africa" and had silhouettes of slaves in chains. He hung out mostly with the popular, snobbish white girls, the skinny blondes, brunettes, and the one cute redhead— Patty Swayne, the only unpretentious one among them— who were cheerleaders for the football team. But he never dated any of them. Why would he date white women, when there were beautiful black women like Niecy.

Niecy was bused in from New Britain. She had silky smooth, dark caramel skin and impeccably unflawed white teeth. She smelled like gardenias and wore a pale red lipstick; her eyelashes were so thick and lustrous I wondered if they were hers or fake. She wore crisply starched dresses every day with polished high heels that exposed the tips of her brightly red-painted first and second toenails. She looked like a model and seemed too glamorous for Newington High. She was round in all the right places, unlike the indistinguishable, homogeneous white chicks.

She was very quiet and kept to herself. I'd see her every day at lunchtime, sitting alone in a corner of the cafeteria with a book in her hand. She never had any food on the table. She was impervious to everyone and everything around her. One time I got my courage up, walked over to her table and plopped down. She politely put her book down and smiled at me with those beautiful white teeth, and I'd suddenly become a bit bashful. "Hi, Niecy; what cha readin'?" "*I Know Why the Caged Bird Sings* by Maya Angelou," she replied, and then looked away somewhat nervously. She wasn't accustomed to having someone sitting or talking with her in the cafeteria. I didn't know who Maya Angelou was; our high school teachers never required books by her, so I asked, "What's it about." I could tell she was shy by the way she bowed her head and shrugged her shoulders when she said, "It's about a young black girl from the South who stops talking, goes mute after her mother's boyfriend molests and rapes her." My mouth fell open and my eyes bugged out. I got nervous. I smiled and said, "Oh, maybe I'll read it someday." She looked up at me as I got up and must have seen the fear and panic in my face because she asked, "Are you okay?" I said, "Oh, yea, I'm just getting hungry; I haven't eaten lunch yet." I waved to her, said, "See ya," and walked outside into the sunlit courtyard and sat on one of the low concrete walls. I felt sick. First, I thought, "Why would anyone write a book about being molested?" But my bigger fear was hearing her say that abhorrent, frightful word "rape." "Would that bastard Bruno try something like that?" I asked myself. My mind starting racing, but the bell rang and I walked to my next class.

There were only a few teachers I really liked or can even remember in high school. My favorite was Mrs. Vasil, my typing teacher who I had a bit of a schoolgirl crush on. She was young and pretty, drove a cream-colored VW Bug and had a great sense of humor and a broad infectious smile; she didn't have a broom-up-her ass like a lot of the teachers did at Newington High. I learned an invaluable, pragmatic skill in her class: touch-typing—using all fingers on the typewriter keyboard, not just the index, and not needing to look at the keyboard. I always went to her room after school and asked if I could wipe down her blackboard. This gave me a chance to ask her questions about being a teacher. I often thought of being a teacher, but didn't really see myself alive in any future context. Mrs. Vasil was kind and patient in answering questions, but I think she knew I just wanted to be in her gregarious yet serene presence.

From Miss Nagy, I learned everything I needed to know about office machines, including a keypunch, an important progenitor to desktop computers. I admired her because she was a no-nonsense, "don't-give-me-that-crap" kind of teacher. She came to Newington High after working several years in an office (she never said where), and her war stories portrayed her as the heroine: "The mimeographic machine broke down in the middle of a big job and I took that machine apart, repaired it and had it running in no time flat," and on and on. Cheryl was in this class with me, and whenever Ms. Nagy launched into one of her stories, we would looked at each other and lower our heads to conceal our laughter. Ms. Nagy was rather fiery in her own special way, even though she still lived at home with her parents, which was not cool at all.

Miss Cyr, my homeroom and English teacher, turned me on to some great literature—Hemmingway, Tennesse Williams, O'Neill, James Baldwin, Gertrude Stein. Miss Cyr was a rather large, tall woman who seemed nervous and unsure of herself. She was not a particular favorite of most students; Nancy and Vicky called her a weirdo. She seemed an outsider and a loner. And, both figuratively and literally, she stood out in a crowd. I admired this about her and found her to be very simpatico. In fact, when I first read O'Neill's *Long Day's Journey Into the Night*, I felt a sense of camaraderie with her; a passage in O'Neill's autobiographical play gave me a shared sense of self:

> "I will always be a stranger who never feels
> at home, who does not really want and is
> not really wanted, who can never belong,
> who must always be a little in love with
> death!"

Of all my high school teachers, the one who may have had the greatest influence on me was my speech teacher, Mrs. Napolitan, who I barely knew throughout high school. I enrolled in her speech class when I was a senior for what I thought would be easy credit. But the class required making speeches in front of the class, and I didn't really have much to say back then. So, I stumbled through with dull, pedestrian accounts of insignificant matters such as why grey was my favorite color, why Black Label was such an impetuous, heady beer, blah, blah, blah. "How droll," is what registered on the faces of my classmates. But, Mrs. Napolitan worked with me, mentored me and inspired me. She believed in me and saw a glimmer of talent that was completely unrecognizable to me. It was the first time in what seemed a very long time that any adult had shown any interest in me for who I was.

Mrs. Napolitan helped to restore some of the confidence in me that had vanished after moving into 96 Hawley Street. She once suggested, "If you don't feel comfortable just talking to your classmates, show them how to do something." I asked, "Like what?" She said,

"Well, do you sew or know any crafts?" I responded, "Sew? I almost flunked out of Home Ec because I couldn't sew a button on a shirt." She laughed. I went on "I'm a pretty good athlete, but I think talking about soccer, basketball or softball would be boring." She said, "What about cooking?" I told her, "I don't know how to cook anything except simple things like hamburgers, hotdogs and orange salads." "Orange salad; what's that?" She asked. I took for granted that the simple Italian recipes I learned from my grandmother and often made as snacks after school could be viewed as epicurean delights by non-Italians. I explained what it was and so one day, with her encouragement, instead of giving a speech, I demonstrated how to make an Italian orange salad. That morning, I packed up my army-issued, canvas green knapsack that I had bought at the Army-Navy store with all the necessary ingredients, and rode my bike to school wondering whether I'd look like an idiot standing in front of class explaining how to make something so simple that a trained monkey could make. When it was my turn I took my time, and patiently explained to the class:

> First you take any type of large orange, preferably with a thick peel. A blood orange is very nice if you can find one; the Sicilian variety is very sweet ("Sorry, Nonni!" I thought to myself). Once peeled, don't just pull apart the slices like a big clod, but cut the orange up into bite-sized pieces. Put them in a bowl. Add some virgin olive oil, the greener the better, Italian parsley, salt and a pinch of oregano. Some people like to add pepper,

but I like it better without. I never learned
to measure the ingredients, so you'll have
to play around with this to suit your own
tastes.

As I made the orange salad, I made certain to make
eye contact at various stages with the students, as Mrs.
Napolitan had taught me. I was almost startled at how
attentive they were to me; and I thought, "Jeez; how
riveting can it be watch someone make an orange salad?!"
Well, what an epiphany. I had them eating out of my
hand (and out of the bowl when I invited them up to
try to finished product. They loved it!). I felt such a rush
of power. Wow, how easy it was to command a group's
attention!

Mrs. Napolitan, more than anyone at the time,
had faith in me. Yet, interestingly enough, she was a
virtual stranger to me. At the end of the school year, she
nominated me for, and I won, the school-wide "Speech"
award. She signed my yearbook for me, and used her
first name, which was rarely done in high school. I'll
never forget her poignant words: "Have a very happy life
and remember, you can do whatever you set your mind
to. Chris Napolitan." I always thought I'd get the "Most
Likely to NOT Succeed" award.

My cousin John was also someone who served as a
coping mechanism for me. He always seemed to be
drifting and floating through life, in his own private little
reverie. Nonni referred to him as "sch-low" (her Italian
pronunciation of "slow") or a "*sbagliorono*" (someone
who never gets it right; a ne'er-do-well). Yet, he had such
a kindness and goodness of heart. He acted more like a

brother to me than Ricci. John looked out for me as much as possible, and referred to me as his little sister. He sort of appointed himself my guardian. And he did a good job of it; and fortunately for me, until I at least looked the legal drinking age—18 was the majority age at the time in Connecticut—and could buy my own booze, John was my supplier of spirits. John had started smoking pot as well and offered to get me some, but I still couldn't tolerate the smell or taste of it.

So I drank. And, at times, I engaged in some exceedingly reckless, intemperate behaviors, such as drinking and driving. I had a few drinking buddies, like Chris Appruzzi, Sue Patrissi and Norma Rhodes—the only other Norma in my high school (maybe city); she was not named after the opera. When I asked her, "Hey, were you named after Bellini's *Norma*?" She responded, "Huh?" I didn't pursue it.

My friends either owned a car—like Norma, who had a cool, 1970 red fastback Mustang—or, like Chris, had access to their parents' colossal, boat-like automobiles. It was the norm for everyone in the car, including the driver, to be shit-faced. This made the Chinese fire drills even funnier to us. We consumed inordinate amounts of Budweiser beer by the quart, cheap wine from screw-top bottles—Boons Farm (Strawberry Hill), Annie Green Springs and Reunite, or my favorite, peach or blackberry brandy. It never occurred to us that we were a danger to others or to ourselves. Such thoughts wouldn't even enter into our frames of consciousness, because at that age, self-absorption precluded consideration of a world outside of us. Moreover, teenagers don't have the perspicacity to see a future; it's all about the present and making ourselves feel good in the present. So, we drink and we drive and we get lost in the unrecognizable, unbeknownst knowledge that we will never again be who we are at this very moment in time.

But, back to John, who was an endless source of entertainment and amusement for my friends and me. He was always throwing wild parties at 96 Hawley when his parents were out and sometimes the police showed up to break them up. He also drove me and my friends up to Springfield, Massachusetts, about thirty-five miles due north of Newington, every other Saturday night for Roller Derby. I especially liked the women's competition where tough women like Joanie Weston would whip around the roller ring flinging their opponents on their asses or over the railings. We would sneak beer or wine in, which seemed to spice up the bawdy entertainment.

But I think John's most brilliant delivery of joy and thrills came from his driving. To say the least, John was a bit of a menace behind the wheel. It wasn't that he would drink and drive, although one could decidedly characterize his driving as such. John was just a bad driver, plain and simple. He wasn't very coordinated and could not seem to focus. And, so, he was perennially dinging, scraping and banging up his 1973 black Pontiac Firebird. He carried a jumbo can of regular black spray paint in his glove compartment, and was forever pulling his car into a well-lit parking lot to spray over the nicks and scrapes before he drove home.

I recall a particularly memorable night after we were leaving the bowling alley on the Berlin Turnpike. Ricci, Billy DeMila, Cheryl and I jumped into John's car after having bowled three games. John started it up, over accelerating as usual, revving up the engine as if he were at the starting line of an auto race. As he was backing out of his parking space, he banged into a car behind him. Then, instead of getting out to see what kind of damage he caused, he proceeded to drive forward, toward his parking space. He drove through his parking space, over the concrete block that serves as a front-wheel marker for parked cars to stop at. The car rocked and lurched into the driving lane of the parking lot. This entire time, Ricci, Billy, Cheryl and I were in absolute hysterics, trying to spit out the words, "John, what the hell are you doing?"

John, concentrating with the intensity of a musician deep into artistic fervor, had the most inscrutable look on his face. He peeled out onto the highway at a ravenous speed; he was driving so fast his wrists, which he rested on top of the steering wheel, were shaking and vibrating quite intensely. And before Ricci, Billy, Cheryl and I could compose ourselves he sideswiped his car on a guardrail. The car was again reeling from the impact as well as our laughter. Shortly afterwards, John pulled into the well-lit parking lot of the Newington Children's Hospital, which is at the base of Newington mountain, about 2 miles from 96 Hawley, and got out to inspect the damage. I had to get out of the car to witness for myself the aftermath of the unbelievable escapade. I was laughing so hard, I barely made it inside to a restroom, just off the abandoned lobby of the Children's Hospital. When I came out, John was hunched over the passenger side of the car with his can of spray paint, scrupulously attempting to mask the damage.

I always resented the fact that my Uncle Bruno had this inane, unfounded rule: boys in his household could get their drivers license when they turned sixteen, girls had to wait until they were eighteen.

"What kind of moronic rule is that?" I asked him. "I've been driving since I was nine-years-old, and I can drive much better than John," which was an understatement.

I still had my passion for driving and cars, especially fast-moving ones, but despite my pleading to get my drivers license, my uncle was unrelenting. As was typically the case with my uncle, the sanctimonious bastard, he never responded, because he believed his rule was law and, therefore, no one was allowed to question him or his motives. He just looked at me with that shit-eating, smug grin on his face.

Ricci was able to get his license when he turned sixteen. My uncle raided Ricci's bank account to buy cars for both Ricci and my cousin John. They each had new Pontiac Firebirds, John's was black, Ricci's deep blue. Ricci would occasionally allow me to drive his car, even though I didn't have my license, because he knew I was a good driver. But as he pulled more and more away from me, he rarely let me drive. So, sometimes, when no one was home and Ricci was out with John in his banged-up, spray-painted Firebird, I would sneak Ricci's spare key and drive around Newington. I wanted to drive more than anything, because it represented a form of freedom to me. A car could take me wherever I wanted to go. No one ever knew I slunk out with Ricci's car (not even Ricci), although, I sometimes hoped that my uncle would see me driving about the town on my own: I planned to honk the horn and flip him the bird, or worse, the *malocchio*, the evil-eye.

I wasn't very interested in boys, but I did have a few boyfriends by the time I was a junior in high school, because most of my girlfriends did. I didn't want to tag along with my friends on their Friday and Saturday night dates. I have a clear memory of one guy I dated, Jim, because he was the first to French-kissed me. We were sitting in the back seat of Steve's car, my friend Nancy's boyfriend. It was about nine p.m. and we were parked in the vacant lot of the Newington Children's Hospital. Steve looked as if he was sucking Nancy's face off. My head was resting on Jim's shoulder and I was trying to talk to him to get his mind (or groin) off of Steve and Nancy making out in the front seat. Then, he suddenly grabbed my face, pulled it toward his, planted his lips on mine and thrust his tongue in my mouth. I yelled, "Get the fuck off of me." He said, "What the fuck's wrong with you, Norma?" I jumped out of the car and told Nancy, "I'm going home." Nancy called out after me and I yelled back, "I'll call you tomorrow." As I was walking home, I thought, "If he wasn't so rough, maybe French-kissing wouldn't be so bad."

Since I seemed uncomfortable with boys, I decided at one point to see if something might be kindled with girls. I didn't really understand the concept of homosexuality, even though I knew two gay men who had lived together for years in a big white house with a built-in swimming pool. Donnie was my Aunt Mary's nephew on her side of the family. He and his partner Lenny had been together for over ten years when I met them. Donnie, who was very feminine, was in his thirties and Lenny was in his late fifties. Donnie had some office job in Hartford and Lenny owned a liquor, or what we call in Connecticut, a package store. Lenny appeared like any other older man to me, not feminine or overly masculine. And, I didn't really stop to think that Donnie was gay because of his femininity, since my brother Johnny was always rather femmy and it never occurred to me that he could be gay. The issue of sexuality was just not in my vocabulary or conceptual framework at the time. And I never heard anyone, not even bloated, bigoted Bruno, make a derogatory remark about Donnie and Lenny.

I invited one of my close friends over one Saturday evening when no one was home. I called her Marshi (short for Marshmallow, a name I bestowed on her because she was such a softie). I plowed her with her favorite drink, Bloody Mary, and attempted to seduce her. What a flop this turned out to be, because she passed out on the living room sofa. Apparently, Bloody Marys are not made up of three parts vodka, one part tomato juice.

I became resigned to the notion that I would never find anyone I could really care about and love in a romantic, intimate way, the way my father loved my mother. It didn't matter I suppose—if you truly loved someone and wanted to share your life with them, it is inevitable that you will be hurt by them; they'll leave you, maybe die.

Despite my inability to date successfully, I was continually trying to fix my friend Cheryl up with someone. Some guy who had already graduated high school, who looked just like Dustin Hoffman, was using her and I thought she deserved better.

The first guy I fixed her up with was Sebby, the town's barber. I met him one day when I was walking through the center of town and he was sweeping the sidewalk in front of his barbershop. He was a short, Italian guy in is late thirties (so he told me, and I believed him), with slicked-back, clean, jet-black, Brylcreemed hair. We started talking, and the next thing you know, I was stopping by to see him when he had no customers. I'd plop down in one of his barber chairs and we'd yack in Italian about the weather or some other banal issue. I missed speaking and hearing Italian. I liked him and also felt sorry for him, because his wife had died not too long before. He also reminded me of my father; not in physical appearance, because Sebby was a puny little guy, where my Dad was tall and stocky. But he was kind, gentle and soft-spoken like my Dad. So, I set him up on a blind date with Cheryl—Cheryl wouldn't talk to me for about a week afterwards. Apparently, they didn't click.

I wasn't about to give up, though. On another occasion, I set Cheryl up on a date with someone I had never met, but he was a friend of Salvatore, the Italian guy I was dating at the time. Sal was a nice guy, but like most Italian men, very possessive. He was engaged to be married to a young, pretty Italian woman, whose picture he still carried in his wallet. He didn't tell me at first why they had broken up.

I liked Sal because he was quiet and very respectful of me. At least for several months. One Friday night when he was dropping me off in his light orange, 1970 MG Midget after a date he tried to feel me up. I promptly slapped his hand off my boob, slapped his face and proceeded to get out of the car. He grabbed my wrist and said, "I'm sorry, Norma. But, it's expected of me." I said, "What the hell are you talking about, Sal? What, because you're a man you have to prove yourself? And, what, you have to test me to see if I can resist? That's bullshit." He said, "I'm sorry, and I won't do it again." I jumped out of the car, went into the house and within ten minutes he had called me from a pay phone to apologize again. He proceeded to tell me that he had broken up with his girlfriend after he finally convinced her to sleep with him. I screamed at him, "You're such a dog! You pester your fiancé to sleep with you, and when she does you dump her because she's 'used goods'; what is it with you guys?" He said, "Well, I want to marry a virgin." I said, "A virgin? What are you nuts?! You're so old-fashioned. And, why is it okay for you to sleep around? The girl has to be a virgin, but the guy can sling his dick around whenever and wherever he likes?" I hung up on him, and took the phone off the hook so he couldn't call back. I broke up with him the next day, not because he put his hand on my boob, but because I thought his values were all screwed up. Sal continued to pursue me, at times stalking me because I had eschewed his advances; he knew I was a virgin and so, I was "wife material." What a nut, I thought. Now this is person who truly belongs in the nut house, not someone like my Dad who did what he did for the right reasons.

Anyway while we were still dating, Sal and I set Cheryl up on a blind date with his friend Vinnie; boy was he the proverbial guinea wop! His hair was slick, oozing with shiny, greasy hair oil. He wore so many heavy gold chains around his neck, it was a wonder he could hold his fat little head up. But the pièce de résistance was his missing front tooth. He had gotten into a brawl the week before and it was knocked out.

We drove to the bowling alley on the Berlin Turnpike; we barely made it. Vinnie had a souped-up black Chevy, and he drove very fast, almost maniacally so. He would drive at an excessively high speed—which only I seemed to like—in the passing lane and if a car happened to be, or got in his way, he would speed up to the car, ride its bumper and start flashing his high beams on and off. Cheryl, who was pressed so closely to the passenger door I thought she would fall out, periodically glanced back at me, glared or scowled, but said nothing. It was the last blind date I would fix her up with.

Act V. Scene 1.
Un Dì, All'azzurro Spazio

("One Day in the Blue Heaven,"
from Giordano's *Andrea Chénier*)

The music is gone for me. There is no Bellini; no Puccini; no Verdi; no Rossini, Donizetti, Mozart, Mascagni, or Catalani. There is no Maria Callas, no Renata Tebaldi, Montserrat Caballé, no Roberta Peters, Beverly Sills, Joan Sutherland, Richard Tucker, Marilyn Horne or anyone else. No one in this house seems to care about any expression of art. I miss the Sunday dinners with my Mom's opera playing in the background, and her teaching me the meaning of, the beauty of opera.

In this house at 96 Hawley Street there is no safety for me; there is no love and no hope. I do not want to live. I pray, now, almost everyday, for God to take me. I pray for the same courage that my father had, to end his pain, misery and disillusionment over this parody of life. But I don't have the courage. I am not afraid of death, but of dying and cannot summon the courage to convey my body to another place, some other place that I know will be better than this. I want more than anything to go back to that place and time when I was surrounded by love and safety and people full of hope—I want and need my beloved parents. It all seemed like a cataleptic dream to me now—my parents, grandparents, aunts, uncles, cousins, the happiness, our home in Torrington. I knew that I would never feel that sense of safety, that sense of home, belonging, constancy and normalcy that I experienced, *lived* in our home in Torrington. Why is everything that is good in life so ephemeral? Is there any lasting presence to happiness? I will never know inviolable trust again.

Run. Why don't I run? I could run away to New York City, or out West, maybe Los Angeles. But I don't run, because a voice from so deep within me—could it be my parents?—tells me that running won't help and it won't save me. Besides, I don't want to leave my Ricci, even though he has completely abandoned me. I knew that as Ricci got older, he would at some point naturally pull away from his baby sister. But, I never expected it to be so harsh, so absolute. I don't think I will make it to my 18th birthday, which seems years away. I am convinced I won't.

I also know that if I leave, the veritable Cruella DeVille, will do everything in her powers to make my life even more miserable. I had continued to ask her if I could live with my grandmother. But, she said as she had on other occasions, "I'll have you put away before that happens."

One evening when I was washing the dinner dishes, I overheard my aunt and uncle, still sitting at the dinner table drinking their espresso, talking about this young teenager from Hartford who had hung himself in his bedroom. His parents were distraught and couldn't fathom why he had taken his own life.

"How awful," I could hear them saying to each other.

"He had such a good life," my aunt was saying, "lived in a nice home with hard-working, respectable parents. What would make a kid do such a thing?"

My uncle responded in his arrogant, moralizing way, "Kids today, they don't know how good they got it; never happy with what they got."

All the while, I was thinking about this poor young guy. There was something more to this picture than what is being portrayed by his parents and the media. Nobody really knows what's going on *inside* a household or *inside* somebody's head. From the outside, it looks safe, sanitized, pristine. But inside, it could be rotting, decaying and festering. Something terrible happened to this young guy, I thought. But, no one will ever know the truth, the real reason that death was a more viable, desirable option than life. Another spirit, I thought, floating through life; another victim of teenage alienation. How do some escape, get spared from this abysmal sense of anger, frustration, loneliness, and despair?

I was envious of him. He was free. And he had the courage to change what was bad or evil in his life. For the first time, I began to understand why my Dad killed himself. And, so I began my love affair with death.

Needless to say, I didn't share my thoughts with my aunt and uncle. After I finished washing the dishes, I went outside, hopped on my bike and went for a long ride.

One day Mary came home to see me crying hysterically, and I wouldn't tell her why. She managed to corner me in the downstairs bathroom, and blockaded the door. She told me I wasn't leaving until I told her why I was crying. I don't know what possessed me to utter the words, "Uncle Bruno touches me." She seemed shocked and almost sympathetic at first; I felt a huge sense of relief for the first time. It felt so good to get this burden off my shoulders. I was able to tell an adult, who was in a position to protect me. But I think in retrospect it must have been self-pity. Her wrath toward me became even more vitriolic.

From this point on, Cruella began telling everyone that I was crazy. She even took me to a psychiatrist, perhaps to prove her point. I didn't protest because I feared she might commit me to the nut house. I went a couple of times to talk to this quack. He was roughly in his mid-forties with steel-grey hair, a mustache and he had a penetrating stare that made me feel very self-conscious. I would clam up, barely answering his insipid, pedantic little questions. He was about as competent as those charlatans who were completely incapable of doing anything to help my Dad.

After two visits, I stopped going. I would take the bus from Newington into Hartford for the scheduled visit, and then call the psychiatrist's office from a phone booth when I arrived in Hartford to cancel my appointment. The bills continued to be sent to, and paid by the bank trustee, Mr. Owen, handling Ricci's and my so-called inheritance. So, no one ever knew I stopped going to the psychiatrist.

Once in Hartford, I would go to McDonald's and buy a hamburger, fries and a chocolate shake to take with me to a place I had recently discovered in my explorations: a deserted, "construction-in-progress" office space on the 8th floor of a building on Main Street. I didn't know or care what was being constructed; it was vacant and quiet. I would sit for hours on the wide, dusty windowsill, gazing out of the filmy, grime-streaked window, eating my food and watching the busy, tidy little world below me.

What is expected of us, our function? To me, it seems like nothing more than an endless series of fatuous, pointless, rote routines: wake up, drink coffee, take shower, go to school, return home, do homework, talk on phone, eat dinner, watch T.V., go to bed. Was there something else? Have I missed the point? Why bother getting up in the morning? Even my Ricci has perished from my purview. He no longer has time for me; he tells me to "Hang out with your own friends," and is angry that I don't show respect to my aunt and uncle. He says, "You're so ungrateful; don't you know how good they are?" He has become very close to Mary; he has fallen under her spell, acceding to her wishes and commands. He doesn't question her like I do. I yell at him, "How can you be so stupid and gullible?" He just flips me the bird, calls me an ingrate and walks away. He won't even fight or "dicker," as my Mom called it, with me anymore. I have lost him. I wish I could tell him about Bruno, but I know instinctively that he will never believe me; he'd say I was making it up and that I was crazy. So I said nothing to him.

It is Ricci's abandonment of me, which is so unspeakably painful, that I finally come to understand those words my mother spoke to me so very long ago:

Più lusinghe, ah, più speranza
presso a morte un cor non ha.

A heart near death
has no illusions, no hope.

I now know for the first time, truly *comprehend* the death
of my parents; I feel the full magnitude of never seeing my
mother or father again; of never feeling their embrace and
the safety of belonging. I know and *feel* my father's pain,
his broken heart, so shattered that he no longer had the
will to live. And, I come to know that hopelessness is the
quintessential human abyss.

What is the point of living out one's life when there is
no hope? When the spirit and soul have been so completely
extinguished that you are nothing but a concentrated mass
of mucus and membranes taking up space? My heart felt
so utterly broken, so near to death, I no longer had the
strength of hope to see beyond each bleary, perfunctory, day.

One night, I was lying on my bed, staring up at the
ceiling, thinking about death. I don't have the courage I
desired. I wanted to be dead, but I didn't want the pain of
death; I grabbed my house key from my knapsack. I began
sawing at my wrists with it. Cheryl once told me that if
you ever get trapped in an alley, use your key as a weapon.
The teeth are almost as sharp as a knife, she had said. But,
it wasn't true. All it did was leave some minor scratches,
which didn't even bleed. I thought of other ways to hurt
myself but I could only muster up the courage to put my
fist through a window on the off chance my writs would
slit open. I thought, "How pathetic you are. You can't even
summon the courage to harm yourself."

For a long time, the two things that had gotten me through even what I thought were the darkest times were my friends and my humor. I was always cracking jokes or finding the humorous side to a serious or even benign situation, just like Nonni Next Door and Nonni Upsatirs. It was one of my kid behaviors that would forever remain frozen in time. And my friends would always laugh. If I had any semblance of life during this period, it was due to the friendship and unspoken love of Cheryl, Nancy, Marshi and Karen, and my cousins John and Nancy. I wish that I could have told them what was happening to me at 96 Hawley Street. But I am too ashamed.

Mostly, my life seemed to be so overwhelmed by complete and utter fear that even my friends—and my old defense of humor—were unable to pull me out of my stupor of angst and the deep sense of loneliness that walled me in. My feisty, ardent spirit that once brought a sense of unwitting aplomb had been choked to death.

Years later I would read something that reminded me of what my life was truly all about back then. It is a passage from Wendy Wasserstein's play, *Uncommon Women and Others*. One of the characters, Rita Altabel, is telling her dorm mates about her recurring dream. She says, "I keep having recurrent *Let's Make a Deal* dreams . . . and my future is always behind the curtain, and the audience is screaming at me, NO, NO TAKE THE BOX! TAKE THE BOX!"

The movie "Godspell" came to town. And it had a fateful impact on me. Karen told me about this rock opera her Mom had read about in the *Hartford Currant* and thought we should go. One Friday night, after we stuffed ourselves with meatball grinders at Newington Grinder we walked to the local cinema in the center of town. The theater wasn't crowded but we walked down to the front row, slouched down in a couple of seats and craned our necks up towards the screen. We talked softly through the previews until someone from the back "shushed" us. We giggled and continued to whisper softly until the movie started. At seventeen, we viewed the "shushers" as crabby old people who forgot what it was like to be young.

The movie opened with the camera first panning across graffiti and then over the skyline of Manhattan bringing the Twin Towers from the World Trade Center into view. John the Baptist, in colorful tails, is walking across the Brooklyn Bridge pulling a cart. The noise from the traffic and pedestrians below and the planes flying overhead crescendos into a scene of bedlam: a traffic jam with cars honking at one another and people screaming out, "Move your car outta there;" "Come on; I ain't got all day." Pedestrians are dodging cars as they are trying to reach their destinations. The camera moves back and forth to different young people who cope with the stress in different ways: a cabby wearing wire-rim glasses, caught in the bottleneck, pulls out a handmade wooden flute and plays a willowy tune. A young black man with a huge afro has a transistor radio earphone in his ear; he's pulling a rack of dry-cleaned clothes through the street; he's oblivious to the noise as he bounces his head to the music only he can hear. Each of the several characters then has a vision of John the Baptist. They are the chosen ones, and follow him to the Bethesda Fountain in Central Park where they frolic in the water and John baptizes Jesus. The group, Jesus' Apostles, now colorfully dressed as hippies, some with painted faces, roves the streets of New York enacting parables from the Gospel of St. Matthew through song, dance and mime.

It wasn't the religious connotations that inspired me (I was still angry with God for taking my parents from me), nor the lyrics. It was the music and the people acting out the story. And, I was completely seduced by their total disregard for convention. I was so captivated by the sense of freedom in these young people, being who they wanted to be in a completely self-assured and unself-conscious manner. "Godspell" was a rock opera, but like the opera I grew up with, the music and story had a hypnotic power over me; they exuded courage and boldness. For the first time since I can remember, I felt that sense of confidence and fearlessness that my parents had instilled in me; that sense of invulnerability and invincibility. The feeling that the only thing I ever had to fear when I was growing up was the occasional scolding or spanking by my Mom. I remember how they made me *feel* about life and living. The feeling is so ethereal, so exceptional that it is virtually indescribable: It's like the magic a kid feels when they still believe in Santa Claus; the euphoria experienced when a kid rides a bicycle for the first time without training wheels; the comfort one feels when your parents take you to the drive-in movies, dressed in your footie pajamas; the warmth and safety a kid feels when they snuggle in bed between their parents after having what they think is their worst nightmare ever. I was getting that back to that place and that time. Now, for the first time since before my parents died, I truly felt hopeful.

I couldn't explain it to Karen. I didn't think she would understand. But, she too was captured by the free-spiritedness of the movie. We went back the next night to see it again.

I told my friend Barbara Porteus about the movie and that she should see it. She was really Ricci and John's friend and was one year older than I, but I occasionally hung out with her because she was cool and had a terrific voice. I think she liked me because she was flattered by the fact that her singing captivated me, and that I was always asking her to sing for me. Barb played the lead singer in one of our high school's productions, "Brigadoon," a fable about a small magical village in the highlands of Scotland that comes alive for only one day every one hundred years. I tried out for a part, but because I had such a terrible voice, I was relegated to the role of a dancer and had to wear an itchy woolen Scottish kilt. It was pretty pedantic but I didn't much mind, though, as long as I could be close to Barb when she was singing. She played the soprano part of Fiona MacLaren. I loved the song "Heather on the Hill," which Fiona reprises, as her beau, Tommy Albright daydreams of her. Tom Serramit got the role of Tommy, but he couldn't sing. Everyone said that he got the part because he was class president.

Ricci had a singing part, too. He played the part of Charlie Dalrymple and performed the solo, "Go Home with Bonnie Jean," a song about the end of Charlie's bachelorhood. Ricci had a beautiful tenor voice. He sounded like Gary Puckett from Gary Puckett & the Union Gap. He could constantly be heard singing, "Young Girl," "Lady Willpower," "Over you" or "Woman, Woman" in the shower. I remember when he went for his audition with the drama director, Mr. Ludlow. I managed to piss him off good by telling him, "If you pretend you can't sing and you don't sing in your natural voice, I'm gonna embarrass you by stopping your tryout." And he knew I'd do it. He didn't say anything to me, since he really did want a part in the musical. John got a supporting role as one of the Scottish townsfolk, and managed to fall off the stage into the orchestra pit during one of the performances bringing the show to a dead standstill until he dragged his carcass back on the stage. When the audience saw that he had not been hurt, there was a tremendous applause. Poor John. Like Nonni said he was a bit of a *"sbagliorono."*

One day, when Barb came over after school, we were sitting on my bed talking about music. I asked her if she knew any arias. She answered by launching into *"Vissi D'Arte"* from *Tosca*. She couldn't remember all the lyrics so she hummed the parts she didn't know.

> *Vissi d'arte, vissi d'amore, non feci mai*
> *male ad anima viva.*
> *Con man furtiva*
> *quante miserie conobbi, aiutai . . .*
> *Sempre con fe sincera,*
> *la mia preghiera*
> *ai santi tabernacoli sali.*
> *Sempre con fe sincera*
> *diedi fiori agli altar.*

I lived for art and love; and I never
harmed a soul.
With a secret hand
I relieved as many misfortunes as I knew of.
Always with true faith
my prayer
rose to the holy shrines.
Always with true faith
I brought flowers to the altar.

I was spellbound. I hadn't heard that aria since before my Mom died. Barb's crisp, unblemished, emotional *a cappella* rendition brought tears to my eyes. I thought of my mother and ran into the bathroom crying. She knocked on the bathroom door, and asked, "Are you okay, Norma." I told her through my tears, "Barb, I'll be right out. Just give me a minute." She asked, "What's wrong?" I replied, "I'll tell you when I come out."

And I did. Barb was the first person I told about my parents. I had never told any of my friends before, but I felt able to tell Barb. Anyone so artistic and gifted that could know and feel my Mom's song had to have the capacity to understand my pain, and most importantly, not judge my father's suicide. She listened, as I told her; she consoled and held me. I couldn't bring myself to tell her about my uncle though, because it was even too perverse for me to comprehend at the time; besides, the one person I tried to tell, Mary, an adult, questioned my credibility and turned on me. But sharing my experience around the death of my Mom and Dad felt so cathartic and freeing. And, it wasn't as daunting as I had expected it would be. My friendship with Barb became extra special, and even after she left Newington a year later to perform in theatrical shows around the country, like "Jacques Brel Is Alive and Well and Living in Paris," a special place in my heart would always be reserved for her.

I slowly brought music back into my life. I had developed an appreciation for various genres of music—especially blues, jazz, soul and R&B, Aretha, the Isley Brothers, Sly and the Family Stone, Ashford and Simpson, Al Green, the Chi-Lites, Harold Melvin and the Blue Notes, Jerry Butler and Tower of Power. While my friends tuned in to the Waspish, Dick Clark's American Bandstand on Saturday afternoons, I much preferred the rhythms of Don Cornelius' Soul Train. I also liked the smooth, rhythmic way blacks danced as compared to whites who stomped around like clods, as though they were trying to put out an errant campfire.

And, I'll never forget the first time I heard Don McLean's "Vincent — Starry Starry Night" on the radio. Not only was the music enrapturing, but the lyrics caught me by surprise. McLean was paying homage to Vincent van Gough, but to me, he wrote the song for my Dad. I went out the next day and bought the album and as I repeatedly played that song, I cried harder with every repetition.

> They would not listen, they did not know how. Perhaps they'll listen now.

> When no hope was left inside on that starry starry night, you took your life as lovers often do. But I could have told you, Vincent, this world was never meant for one as beautiful as you.

I instinctively knew, from the very first moment I became conscious of it playing in the background, that opera would always be the window to my soul. It was, I knew, extant during my gestation. It was time to fold opera back into the person who I was.

Opera was a gift from my mother, passed down to her from her mother. She taught me the meaning, the beauty of opera; its power to ease the mind, rest the soul, eddy the heart, and nurture the spirit. The irony of opera is almost comic; that out of the depths of such tragedy—the misery, despair, suicide and death which characterize it—such brilliant, majestic sounds reveal themselves. It exposes one's spirit. My grandmother was absolutely correct; the lyrics of opera can be quite compelling, as I came to know from *Norma*. However, the glory of opera can especially be found in the music; it is the music that transfixes me, empowers me, transports me to a state of absolute grace.

How could anyone listen to Puccini's hypnotic "Non Piangere Liu" from *Turandot* and not be completely enthralled at the very moment that Calaf, Liù and Timur, in an operatic fugue, lift their voices with the leitmotif as it swells and crescendos, the thundering of the kettledrums and the crashing of the cymbals exploding throughout every corpuscle of the body? It doesn't really matter what is being said at that very moment of anticipation and culmination. The mélange of voice, melody and instrument—wind, string and percussion—satiate the body, mind and soul.

Listening to opera now takes me back, back to another place and time when there was extraordinary happiness and trust in my life. The music helps me to recapture my past; teaches me how to evoke the goodness, the safety, joy and hope that once prevailed; it helps me to pull the elements from my past life into my present, to heal and to move on.

I know it is them. It is clear to me now and I can see it, almost omnisciently, for I am alive. It is my mother and my father. Their love for me, confidence in me, and hopes for my destiny, adorn me; emancipate me. And what they taught me—not through any spoken words about the power of hope and love—invokes a capacity so strong, that I know I will survive. I know the truth. I can hear the words that Maddalena sings in Giordano's "*La Mamma Morta*" (My Mother is Dead):

Fu in quel dolore
Che a me venne l'amor!
Voce piena d'armonia,
e dice: "Vivi ancora! Io son la Vita!
Ne' miei occhi è il tuo cielo!
Tu non sei sola!
Le lagrime tue Io le raccolgo.
Io sto sul tuo cammino
e ti sorreggo!
Sorridi e spera! Io son l'Amore!

It was during that sorrow
that love came to me!
A voice filled with harmony
and said: "Live still! I am Life!
In my eyes is your heaven.
You are not alone!
I gather your tears.
I walk along your path
and sustain you!
Smile and hope! I am Love!

Act V. Scene 2.
Ridi Pagliaccio

("*Laugh then, Clown*," from
Leoncavallo's *Pagliacci*)

As Ricci pulled more and more away from me, my brother Johnny and I became closer. It was ironic because Johnny and I were never very close growing up; for one thing, there was a three-year age difference, which seemed exponentially larger when we were kids, but also, he didn't seem to like my audacious, carefree, defying ways. Besides, he always allied himself with adults, and was forever seeking their veneration. I loathed this type of behavior. It was so smarmy.

Now, however, we were both older, in age and in spirit. He was 19 and in college; I was 16, and in high school. And separately, through our own distinct paths, we had both grown and matured since we last lived together, as brother and sister, those many years ago in our home in Torrington.

By the time he had started college, Johnny had severed his contact with Mary and Bruno. Mary, in her typical power-wielding ways, put my poor brother through hell. After he had completed his junior year of high school in Torrington, Johnny wanted to remain there to finish his senior year. My aunt told him she would not approve of this, that he would have to return to Newington to finish out high school. Johnny dared to contravene her edict, so she initiated court proceedings to *force* him to return to the domain of his legal guardians at 96 Hawley Street. The probate judge who was assigned the case obviously did not see the rationale behind this and so he opined in Johnny's favor, providing he had someplace to live in Torrington. Since my Aunt Mary had mysteriously worked something out with Uncle Livio and Auntie Pauline so that they wouldn't take him back into their home, Johnny went to live with my paternal grandmother's cousin, Guiditta, her husband Eugenio and their eldest daughter, *Enrighetta* (Henrietta), who legally renamed herself Anna (as soon as she possibly could, not surprisingly), in their modest Torrington home.

Nonni Upstairs and Guiditta had become close friends over the years, in fact closer than the friendship between Guiditta and Nonni Next Door who were first cousins. These two old Italian women put their feisty, determined heads together and made a compact. The bond of friendship was its seal—it required no social security checks, no financial remuneration, no "what's-in-it-for-me" arrangement. The Bacconi's, who my paternal grandparents had sailed with to America in 1914, had now created a safe home for my brother Johnny, which enabled him to not only finish out his last year of high school in Torrington, but to also sow the seeds of a lifelong, intergenerational bond between the Riccucci's and the Bacconi's.

I came to appreciate the characteristics in Johnny that I found wimpy and foppish when we were children—honesty, gentleness and kindness. It is often the case that as we get older, we come to see in our siblings, whether older or younger, their virtue in a clearer, richer light.

When Johnny went home to Nonni's flat in Hartford during his breaks from Southern Connecticut State College he would always invite me to spend time with him, taking me out to do fun things—movies or shows at the Bushnell Theater in Hartford, or even better, in New York City. At my grandmother's exhortation, John majored in Italian at Southern Connecticut, but his true passion was for the theater and so, he minored in drama. To my good fortune, he was enamored with theater, especially the glittering, elaborate musicals that were mounted on Broadway. One Saturday in the fall of 1973, John took me to see 2 shows, a movie and the Rockettes at Radio City Music Hall. We took a bus in from Hartford and first saw a movie at Radio City; it was "Ash Wednesday" with Elizabeth Taylor and Henry Fonda. It was about a middle-aged very vain woman trying to save her marriage by getting a face-lift. At the same time she's contemplating having an affair with a young guy. It mostly seemed like drivel to me, except the part where they showed some of the surgery, and how subcutaneous fat is removed to perk up the skin under Liz Taylor's (or her character, Barbara's) eyes. I read in the playbill that what we were really looking at was chicken fat. It was fascinating in a very gross way.

The movie was followed by the Rockettes lined up in perfect precision, dancing to loud, kitschy music like Ethel Merman's "Everything's Coming Up Roses." As they kicked up their legs high in the air in complete unison, I turned to Johnny and whispered in his ear, "This reminds me of the June Taylor dancers we used to watch with Mommy and Daddy on the Jackie Gleason show. Remember how they would lie on the floor in circles, with their shoulders touching and with the camera overhead they made kaleidoscopic patterns by moving their arms and legs together?" He turned to me with a big broad smile across his face, and he squeezed my arm. It was one of those magic moments when you capture something real special from the past.

After pizza and soda at some dive in Times Square, we then went to a matinee of "Sleuth," with Patrick Macnee, from "The Avengers." I loved watching the reruns of that show, because of the strong role it created for a woman the British Agent, Emma Peel played by Diana Rigg. "Sleuth" was a mystery with all sorts of twists and turns about an older man trying to trap and kill a younger man who is having an affair with his wife. It was pretty riveting and kept me at the edge of my seat for most of the play.

Johnny took me to dinner at Mamma Leone's, a cheesy joint on West 44th street that attracted tourists who had probably never eaten a meatball in their lives. He said, "It's an institution in the City, so even if the food is no where as good as Nonni's, you have to try it for the experience." I asked John, "So, who and where is Mamma Leone." He said, "She's dead; a conglomerate bought the place out a long time ago." We ordered ziti with sweet Italian sausage that was served it humongous pasta bowls, and it tasted like the chef scooped it out of a big industrial-sized can and shoved it in the oven on high.

After dinner, we saw Michelle Lee in Cy Coleman's "Seesaw." It was a brassy musical about some podunk lawyer from the Midwest who falls for a flighty, kooky, dancer from the Bronx. I loved the colorful music but the story was on the insipid side. By the time the show let out it was after 11 p.m. It was a full day and I was looking forward to recounting the fun events with John on the bus ride back to Hartford, but I fell asleep.

The entire day was the inception of my abiding love for the theater—plays, musicals, dramas, and comedies. I was so grateful for having Johnny back in my life.

Johnny always invited Ricci to join us on our excursions, but he showed no interest; he wanted no contact with Nonni or Johnny. This was how Aunt Mary wanted it, and Ricci acceded, as he always did. I wasn't about to give either of them up for Cruella DeVille or anyone else. So, I maintained contact with both, and suffered the vituperative consequences from Ricci. At some point I said to myself, "tough shit," Ricci would find something wrong with *anything* I did so, what the hell, I'll stop trying to please him.

I enjoyed spending time with Johnny and getting to know him better. I wasn't sure if we had both changed a lot, or if we were seeing things differently now that we were older and had shared the mutual experience of losing our parents and, then, of independently salvaging the remains after the fallout. Whatever the case, I knew that I not only loved him, but I really liked him. He was like my father in many ways—kind, considerate, selfless and simpatico. Those days when he would sneer at me or tattle on me to my mother or grandmother seemed so very long ago. It almost seemed as though they were part of a different, yet familiar lifetime. Now, I wish that I could be the one tattling—on my uncle. I wish I could tell Johnny what is happening; maybe he can take me away from here. But I say nothing to him; nothing to anyone. Who would believe such a thing especially about my uncle, the pillar of the community? Everyone loved him. Even all the high school students, because he was the class photographer; they called him Bruno. He had the Newington High School contract to take pictures of all sporting events, school outings, plays and portraits for the school yearbooks. I always wondered if he molested any of the students as they posed for their yearbook pictures.

So how could I tell Johnny? I'd be put away in a nut house with crazy people, just like my father was. I'd be given shock treatment, maybe a lobotomy. It still seemed senseless to reveal my secret to Johnny or anyone else.

I come to realize that I not only did not love my uncle, but I very much disliked him. And, it wasn't just the pedophilia that made him such an objectionable, despicable human being. For one thing, he was profoundly prosaic; granted he had an artistic streak that manifested in his profession as photographer, but this unidimensional side was not enough to balance the banality and dull-wittedness he embodied. In fact, the Riccucci's always said Bruno had no business sense, and if weren't for my father loaning him large sums of money, he would have never made it as a photographer. Even Nonni Upstairs, his own mother, had to bail him out on those occasions when his electricity would be shut off for failing to pay his bill. "*Che vergogna,*" how shameful, she would say.

I often wondered how Uncle Bruno wound up in the same crop of kids with my mother and Uncle Corrado.

They were smart, witty and fun. My Uncle Corrado went on to earn a doctorate of engineering at the University of Bologna, and worked most of his life as an engineer on small business machines at a medium-sized factory in Arezzo, just 10 miles Northwest of Cortona.

My mother wasn't formally educated, having to quit school after the seventh grade, but she read a lot and knew a lot. She had a quiet intellect that was heuristic, and she could converse on just about any subject matter, especially music.

My Uncle Bruno, on the other hand, struck me as being somewhat illiterate. He was a dark, brooding man, who had this superior air about him, and the accompanying reticence that goes with narcissistic, imperious behavior. And when he did make some declaration, it was vacuous. Like the time he learned about the act of vandalism against Michelangelo's Pietà, the statue in the Vatican showing Mary holding the dead, limp body of Jesus after the crucifixion. Claiming he was Jesus Christ, some nut job took a hammer to Mary's face and arm. "That idiot should have his balls cut off," Bruno said assuredly. I quizzically looked over at him and thought, "*Your* balls should be cut off, you pervert. You have no ability, no right to judge right from wrong." He apparently thought defacing a statue, granted a beautiful work of art by Michelangelo, was a heinous crime, but his depravity was perfectly normal.

But I think the actual reason why Bruno didn't talk much was because he was just plain dumb. To say he wasn't skilled in the art of conversation is a gross understatement. As a matter of fact, I never saw him or even his wife ever reading a book. The only literature that seemed to pique their vapid minds was found in dirty magazines, secretly hidden away under their mattress. (My cousin Nancy came across them one day in her ritual snooping. What was she looking for anyway?) Bruno was an imposter, who had managed to delude everyone. Maybe he was the one, aberrant consequence of the inbreeding of the Manciati clan—his grandparents were, after all, first cousins. No matter; what a bumfuck, I thought.

But I think the most confounding, say duplicitous aspect about Bruno is that he would never fart in front of us, like my Dad did. This was too crude and crass for his noble character and nature. Apparently farting was improper and indecent but molestation was completely within his realm of dignified behavior.

Working became a refuge of sorts to me. I started babysitting when I was fourteen, and at fifteen, I was hired as a waitress at Grant's Bradford House. In Connecticut, at the time, one could work at the age of fifteen, with parental, or in my case guardian, consent. I loved the interaction with my co-workers and the customers, and found myself sitting at the counter after hours sipping coffee and chatting with whoever was on duty that day or evening.

There was one waitress that always fascinated me. Her name was Doris. She was very seasoned, in her early 50's with thinning, frightfully reddish orange hair. She always had a lit cigarette hanging out of the corner of her abundantly, flaming scarlet lipsticked mouth. I was forever finding smudged ashes on the lunch counter and tables I bussed for her, a task I readily agreed to since we had very different ideas of cleanliness. I started carrying beverage orders on a small tray only to encourage her to do the same; no matter how many glasses of soda, juice, milk or water she carried, she found it necessary to plunge her dirty, nail-bitten fingers inside the beverages to grasp the glasses as she served them to her customers.

My boss, Mr. Barnes was from Jamaica. He was tall, thin and very handsome. I didn't realize that he liked me until after I had quit. I was having coffee with some of my former co-workers at the luncheonette counter just before I left, and Mr. Barnes beckoned me over. He asked me if I wanted to go out on Friday night. I told him no, because first he wasn't a boy, he was a man. I thought, "What on earth would he want to take me out for?" I was too young. I was also afraid of men, so there was no way in hell I would date him. But I thought that it was respectful of him not to hit on me while I was working. I didn't know what "sexual harassment" was at the time, but he sure could have made my tenure at Grant's awful.

Just before I turned sixteen, I started working at Kinney Manufacturing, which manufactured various types of plumbing parts. The job was part-time and was arranged through the Newington High work-study program. I earned high school credit for working; instead of taking afternoon classes, like the college-bound students, I went to work and learned basic office skills and how to get a payroll out on time. The front office space I was assigned to had about eight other women doing administrative or clerical work.

My good friend Cheryl was one of them, and we were quite the pair. While we were good at and serious about our jobs, we talked and laughed a lot when the bosses weren't around. Like the time we were working overtime one Saturday. None of the office supervisors were around, only the shop foremen. Cheryl went out to the shop floor to deliver inventory forms to one of the foremen, Joe Bouchè, and while she was out there, I got on the intercom system which projected through the entire shop and announced in a very calm, sexy voice, "Table, paging chair; table, paging chair; please dial 69." Cheryl ran back into the office laughing hysterically. I asked, "Did anyone laugh?" Barely able to compose herself she said, "Everyone just stopped what they were doing and stared up at the speaker, totally confused and Joe asked me, 'What the hell is that?'" She said, still laughing, "Norma, I could kill you; I almost peed my pants out there."

We liked the receptionist Beverly Zaleski a lot because she always got our jokes and never chased us away when we sat with her in the reception area. Beverly was in her early thirties; she was very petite and cute with her frosted blond hair and perky nose. She was Italian, too. Her husband Roger, a salesman for some other company, occasionally stopped by to visit her; he was cute, too, but had the worst posture I'd ever seen. I felt a closeness to Beverly because she had a lot of the same qualities as my Mom: kind, warm, affectionate, gentle and caring. I never told Beverly directly that I was very unhappy living at 96 Hawley Street, but she seemed to know. She could see it in my eyes and read it in my behavior. She once asked me, "What's all your humor and joking around a cover for?" I'd make a face, a fart sound with my mouth, a twist of my body and skipped away. At least it made her laugh.

Cheryl didn't much like my direct supervisor, Mrs. Hamilla, who was an old, unfriendly, stern woman, with chronic bad breath. Yet, for some inexplicable reason, she took a liking to me, even taking me under her wing. She was very kind to me, and imparted all sorts of practical knowledge about bookkeeping and accounting. And even though I was totally blown away at the time, she told me it was never too early to start a retirement account! But, most importantly, she gave me fundamental skills about managing my own business affairs that would prove invaluable in adulthood.

I really liked the people I worked with; except for one young woman, about Cheryl's and my age, who was also a part-timer. Her name was Sharon, and she was a short, stocky smudge of a person, almost dwarf-like. She had the type of personality that managed to grate everyone's nerves. The one thing she did that was a taboo in any office was try to be the "boss' pet." She liked putting her nose up the assess of supervisors by doing such things as trying to get Cheryl and me in trouble for talking. "Mrs. Hamilla," she would shriek in her whiny tone, "Norma and Cheryl are goofing around again." Most of the time we ignored her, but sometimes I just couldn't resist baiting her. I remember one afternoon when she came into work, she was walking around her desk, bragging about how good she was at karate, and how she was able to flip men much larger than herself. She would soon have her black belt, she boasted.

I looked at Cheryl, winked, and then turned to Sharon and asked, "Do you think you could flip me, even though I'm much taller than you?"

"Piece of cake," she assuredly responded.

So, there we were in the middle of the office, testing her mastery of karate. Before she could even come out of her doddering-little karate stance, which made her look as though she were on the threshold of taking a great, big dump, I flipped her, and her big butt thumped so loudly on the ground, my desk shook. Cheryl laughed so hard, she was doubled over, clutching her stomach. The other office workers also laughed, because no one in the office much liked Sharon. Mrs. Hamilla wasn't there; even though she didn't like Sharon, she would not have approved of such antics. I felt a little bad about it afterwards, but it provided a serendipitous moment to provoke some laughter during an otherwise dull day. Besides, people who crowed so loudly about themselves got on my damn nerves.

My cousin Nancy married her fiancé, Artie, who drank too much and was always flirting with my friends, especially Nancy Jutras. She would be moving out of 96 Hawley Street into a small, one-bedroom, country-furnished apartment over a farmhouse about 8 miles away. It was distressing to see her leave, but, fortunately for me, my cousin Claudia was separating from her husband Danny, who had become physically abusive, and was moving in with her three-year-old son Michael. It wasn't as though I was happy that her marriage was falling apart; and, I was appalled that she had fallen victim to domestic violence. I was just relieved to know that I wouldn't be alone at night in my bedroom. Although my Uncle had never been successful in sneaking into my room during the night, I lived in constant fear that he would. But, now Claudia and Michael slept in the queen-sized bed next to me; and every night, Michael was in bed by nine. So, I felt some sense of relief because although my Uncle was a dumb-fuck, he wasn't that dim-witted to risk coming up to our bedroom with Michael there.

I became very attached to Michael, and he in turn to me. Claudia starting going out a lot at night even during the week, and so I was assigned the task of babysitting Michael. I welcomed this, because he was such a good kid. Besides, by the time Claudia left for the evening it was close to Michael's bedtime. He'd sit and watch T.V.

with me after dinner, and never argued or sulked when I said, "Almost time for bed; let's go wash your face, and brush your teeth." I liked reading him bedtime stories and watching his tiny little eyelids fight to stay open. I'd give him a tiny kiss on his forehead before tiptoeing out of the room.

I did, however, have some arguments with Claudia and especially Mary about having to baby-sit on the weekends. "Claudia is going out Saturday night, so you have to babysit Michael," she would say. "But, I have plans," I would respond. "Why is it my responsibility to cancel my plans? Claudia's his mother," I unsuccessfully pleaded my case. "Because Claudia wants to go out; anyway you have to do what I tell you to do." There was never any point in disputing her warped sense of logic. She was the boss.

I started having my friends over on Saturday nights, since every Saturday night, Mary and Bruno were out visiting friends or at some event sponsored by the Knights of Columbus or the Kiwanis Club, of which my Uncle was "upstanding" members of. They never got home before midnight. We would listen to music, dance and drink beer or cheap wine that my cousin John procured for us. Even though Ricci was still aloof, he, John and Billy DeMila would occasionally invite their friends over and we'd have unruly parties, where the weak-bellied, like Karen, would puke for some reason in pretzel or Cheez Doodles' bowls or in the small evergreen shrubs that framed the front of the house. Once a group of us played spin the Lazy Susan, our version of spin-the-bottle. Chris Appruzzi came up with the idea. We'd put a kitchen utensil like a spatula on the wooden, rotating tray and spin it. Chris, who was short, plump, had stringy dull hair and greasy, pockmarked skin had an enormous crush on John. She would intently watch as the tray spun around and around, hoping it would land on John, who prayed that it wouldn't. John liked my friend Cheryl and sat in anticipation of a smooch from her. But, Cheryl had a crush on Ricci, who seemed happy to kiss any of my friends. Although still a virgin, Ricci was quite the ladies man at this point, tall, thin, cleared up acne, and styling a robust Afro. He was one of those Italian guys with curly, nappy hair; he got so tired of hot combing it every morning that he finally decided to let it go natural and poof, he had a gigantic, thick, Afro. He would have been a real *gumba* had he worn silk shirts unbuttoned to the chest, exposing shiny gold chains around his neck. The only boy I was even remotely interested in kissing was Bill. But, to avert the risk of the spatula landing on some geek, I always forfeited my spin to Cheryl. Besides, I was more interested in and fascinated by the drama created by this simple circular household gadget that beckoned such eagerness and expectancy of affection that might or might not be met with great enthusiasm.

Every half-hour or so, I would check in on Michael. I don't know why I tiptoed up the stairs and into the bedroom, because the noise from the music and rowdy drunkards was so loud, it reverberated through the entire house. But all the while, Michael slept peacefully and safely through it all.

I got to know Claudia a little better after she moved back in with her parents. And, I developed an appreciation for her kooky, irreverent ways, like when she adopted an adorable female puppy for a short period of time. It was jet black and she called her Beulah, after the black maid in the 1950s sitcom of the same name. I didn't know whether to laugh or call her a racist (which she was not!). She had to give Beulah up after a couple of months, though, because she chewed up everything in sight.

Claudia was also the only one who stood up to Bruno. I think she sometimes contradicted him just to be confrontational, and I liked this. And, he certainly could be relied upon for one thing: making stupid remarks, like when he made a sexist comment about Ella Grasso, a Democratic politico from Connecticut who at the time was a representative of the U.S. Congress and would eventually become Governor of the state. "Women belong in the kitchen," Bruno declared dryly and tritely. And I could count on Claudia to jump all over him for saying something so idiotic. And, because she was clearly his favorite, he just listened, and never reprimanded her for defying him, as he would have for anyone else.

Claudia was also simpatico, maybe because she was capable of remembering, unlike many adults, the anomie of being a teenager. She was about nine years older than I; but to a sixteen year old, she was a grown up. And she helped me out of same bad jams. Like the time I came home one Friday night so drunk I barely made it up the stairs and to the toilet bowl. I don't remember much of what happened, because I passed out with my head still in the toilet. I do remember Claudia pulling my head out of the bowl, and sitting me on the edge of the tub. She gently washed my face with a warm washcloth, helped me on with my P.J.'s and put me to bed. I always wondered if I would have drowned in my own vomit had she not rescued me.

Claudia would also cover for me, Ricci and John whenever something went wrong with one of our wild parties. One Sunday morning after a real binger the Newington cops showed up at 96 Hawley Street. It was about 11:30 in the morning and we were sitting in the living room drinking coffee, nursing our hangovers. Mary and Bruno had already left for the day, visiting friends of theirs in Hartford. We saw a cop car pull up in front of the house, not thinking anything of it. When the doorbell rang, John answered the door, and one of the cops asked, "Did you have a party here last night?" Claudia looked at us with a frown on her face, and Ricci's and my eyes bugged out. We heard John say, "Hold on." He ran into the living room and said frantically, "The cops are here." We sent Claudia to the door to deal with them, not knowing what we had done wrong. Apparently, someone at our party put sugar in the gas tank of another's car, which clogged up the engine, ultimately demolishing it. We could hear Claudia lying to the cops, explaining that it must have been a random act of violence, because she had had a quiet party at the house that night and no one complained of problems. The cops left but Claudia was pissed at us, yelling, "What the fuck went on here last night?" We found out the next day that two young women at the party had a fight over not a guy, but another woman. The row apparently ended when one of the women vandalized her competitor's car. Needless to say, they didn't get invited back to any of our parties.

I felt a special connection with Claudia when she told me about a dream she had after her miscarriage. Claudia's first pregnancy was a difficult one, and she ultimately miscarried. She went into a depression afterwards, but something happened to help her break out of the bondage of despair. She told me that one night she had a dream of my mother sitting in our living room in Torrington in her black Boston Rocker, completely veiled in black lace with the smallest of eyelets. She was surrounded by African Violets, my Mom's favorite flower, and enfolded in her arms, was the dead body of Claudia's unborn child. It gave me the chills; I, like Claudia believed my Mom was telling her that everything would be all right. I thought that there must have been something singularly extraordinary about Claudia for my Mom to have intervened as she had.

About a week before I started my senior year in high school, I was clearing the dinner table after everyone had gotten up and left the room except for my uncle. I did something so extemporaneous that it came as a shock even to me; yet it seemed to reflect the very essence of the person I was growing into. I was a few months away from my seventeenth birthday. I would be eighteen in a year, and no longer bound, legally or financially, to Bruno and Mary. This, along with the confidence I had regained in recent months, gives me hope and strength. I sat down in a chair next to my uncle, who was sitting at the head of the table, and looked him directly in the eyes. His face registered inquisitiveness, maybe surprise, because I'd always kept my distance from him. I never got physically close to him like this. His eyes were bloodshot and his breath smelled sour from his cheap wine. I said in a very cool, unfaltering manner, "I don't want you trying to bother me anymore."

He studied my face for what appeared to be longer than Sunday mass, eyes frenetically darting about trying to read me, figure me out. He finally responded, "Okay."

I thought, *La commedia è finita*, (the comedy has ended), as Canio utters his final line in *Pagliacci*.

I think he saw something in my eyes; a young woman that would no longer tolerate his bullshit; someone who had consummately woken up from a deep, comatose sleep to take ownership of herself. I think he was actually afraid of what he saw. Although I had no intention of directly telling anyone about what he had done to me all these years—because of the shame I felt and that no one would ever believe me anyway—I was unafraid of him now. He could no longer hurt me; he no longer had power over me. I believe that he knew, deep within, that I had power over him; the power of truth.

ACT V. SCENE 3.
UN BEL DI VEDREMO

("*One fine day we will see each other again*,"
from Puccini's *Madame Butterfly*)

It was November 20th, 1974. I realized by now that perhaps the other shoe had dropped, but somehow I seemed to have survived it. That I was eighteen and still alive was a testament to my parent's capacity to love, sustain and believe in me. It's been over six years since my Mom died, and over four since my Dad made his fateful decision to follow her. I miss them, and wish they were here. I see them now only in my dreams; but even in my dreams, they come to me less and less.

So, this was it; I was on my way. I was saying goodbye to a significant piece of my past and feeling weighed down by the sadness of it all. I wasn't quite sure where I was going, but I knew it would be to somewhere safer, cleaner. I wondered whether I would make the right choices in life. And I felt challenged by a conflict that had developed deep within me—part of me wants to personify the goodness of my parents; carry forth the probity, the decency which so characterized their short lives. But my life has been irrevocably altered; I feel cynical, distrustful. An inner voice tells me to break from the embittered outlook that often consumes me, but I am afraid of returning to that state of innocence, where I will once again be betrayed by the cruelty and evil that periodically—or invariably—surfaces in every one of us. Who could I trust? Should I suspect everyone?

I wondered what my life would have been like had my parents not died. I'd have graduated Torrington High School and would have been enrolled in college somewhere. Would my parents have been proud of me? What would their hopes for me have been? I would have wanted to make them proud of me. Despite the uncertainty of my destiny, I will be driven by this goal for the rest of my life.

I took what little was left of my so-called inheritance, that which had not been plundered by family members, including Mary and Bruno's squandering on such amenities as trips to Italy, aluminum siding for their house, yearly trips to Atlantic City, new cars—like the new Lincoln Continental with the "suicide doors," where the rear car doors open in the opposite of the regular direction just like old British cars—and I bought a sports car: a four-on-the-floor Triumph TR-6, plum, with tan leather interior and a tan convertible top. Through it all, I still had my passion for cars and for driving—in this case, away, as fast as I could; it was all I wanted.

I had also saved an incidental amount of money from my job at Kinney Manufacturing. After graduating in June, I started working full-time and was earning minimum wage, $2 an hour. Cheryl had already left for a good job at

Aetna Insurance in Hartford, so it was pretty dull working all day without her. But, work was still a sanctuary and I welcomed the opportunity to continue honing my business skills under the tutelage of Mrs. Hamilla.

My Aunt somewhat depleted the small amount of savings I had earned that summer by charging me rent. Once I graduated high school, she no longer received survivor's social security benefits on my behalf. She was still receiving Ricci's benefit, since he was enrolled in Manchester Community College; back then, the benefits were paid to survivor's guardians up until the age of 21, providing they remained in school. I thought, "What a dummy. She insisted that I not go to college, but now she probably wishes that I had; then the gravy train would have kept rolling."

I was ready to leave 96 Hawley Street the day I turned eighteen. But, Ricci told me I should wait until after the holidays, out of respect for Mary and Bruno. He still didn't get it: I was leaving *because* of them. Maybe someday he would know, believe me and understand. So, I waited until after the New Year, only to appease Ricci.

I knew I'd never see Cruella DeVille or the Marquis de Sade again, and this knowledge soothed my spirit, soul, and mind tremendously. However, I was very sad about leaving Ricci, even though he had completely blotted me out of his life. Nor did I know at this point in time that he would not want to see or speak to me again for almost twenty years. The only thing I could do for him now was pray to my parents to guide, direct and aid him on his way. I found comfort in the fact that I still had Johnny and my Nonnina, and I knew inherently that they would always be there for me. And I knew that the vivid memories and experiences of my wonderful childhood would carry me through any adversity I would encounter.

My cousin Nancy was having marital problems with her husband, Artie, so I don't think my saying goodbye really registered with her. And Claudia had moved to Las Vegas that summer after I graduated. I accompanied her to help with Michael while she looked for a place to live and work. It was the first time I had ever been on a plane. I was excited about it, and loved the speed of plane as it barreled down the runway and gracefully lifted itself off the ground. I was peering out the small window and watched as the earth got smaller and smaller. But, just as the plane was reaching the clouds it tilted sideways, turning very abruptly in another direction and I started feeling very nauseous; everything started to spin. I tasted the vile, sour bubble as it rose from my stomach to my throat. Holding a hand over my mouth, I garbled out to Claudia, "I think I'm gonna to puke." She leaned toward me, pulled a small white bag the size of a lunch sack from the seatback in front of me and handed it to me. I fixed my gaze on it, quickly shot her a disgusted glance, and had just enough time to unbuckle my seatbelt and make it to the toilet. While I was barfing, a stewardess was knocking on the door saying, "Miss, you must take your seat during takeoff." She kept banging and yelling, "Miss; miss." After I washed my face and rinsed my mouth out with cold water, I emerged from the tiny closet-like toilet to a very angry stewardess. Before she could reprimand me any further I said rather flatly, "Lady, if you think I was gonna barf in a bag, you'd have to carry me off this plane in a straight jacket." She just glared at me as I staggered back to my seat. Claudia said sympathetically, "Guess we should have gotten you some Dramamine." At least she didn't call me "vomit."

But the hardest part of this trip was having to say goodbye to Michael when it was time for me to return to Connecticut. As Claudia, Michael and I were walking to my gate, Michael followed close behind me holding on to my back pocket with his tiny little hand, as he always did when we went for walks. When we got to the gate, I started crying because I didn't know when I'd see them again. Claudia was holding Michael at that point, and when I reached over to give him another kiss goodbye, Michael was crying, stretching his arms and tiny little body out to me, as if to say, take me with you. We had gotten so close that neither one of us wanted to separate. But, it was inevitable.

The Dramamine put me to sleep for most of the plane trip back to Connecticut. I remember thinking before dozing off that I didn't want to ever get close to anyone again, because I didn't like the pain of losing them; nothing really lasts forever anyway. I also told myself that I would never, ever have children because I wouldn't want to leave them or have them go through what I had gone through after my parents left me.

When I told Nonni I was leaving, she was not at all pleased. On the one hand, she implicitly understood my desires to vacate the premises of *quel buco nero*. "But why was I planning to drive aimlessly around the country, *come una vagabonda* (like a gypsy)?" she wanted to know. And, why did I waste my money on an impractical sports car? *Che scema* (SHAY-mah); *che vergogna*. Because my obstinate, resolute personality so mirrored that of my grandmother's, which she herself would come to acknowledge, I was spared the operatic drama of an old Italian woman maniacally sobbing and hurling herself (figuratively anyway) over the balcony of her tiny flat in Hartford. I had just seen "Amarcord," Fellini's semi-autographical account of his coming of age and couldn't get the hilarious image out of my head of his mother, who copes with the escapades of her young son by screaming histrionically, "*Mi ucciderò*" (I'll kill myself).

I learned many years later that Nonni didn't think I would ever return to Connecticut. She must have underestimated her own power. It was the power of strength, wisdom, love and truth that would always draw me back to her. She would forever be home to me.

My brother John gave me a small medal of St. Christopher, the Patron Saint of Travelers, for my car. Part of me wanted to chuck it in the trash because I was still mad at the whole lot of them: Jesus, God, and Saints Ping, Pong and Pang, as Puccini called them in *Turnandot*. Except, I find that I can still pray to the Blessed Virgin Mary. Well, I know she is the Mother of Jesus, and that she is blessed, and that her name is Mary. But, I'm not real sure that she is a Virgin. It doesn't matter, though; I feel that I can pray to her. I always liked this passage from *Paradiso*, Dante's final part of *La Divina Commedia*:

> You are for us the noonday torch of charity,
> and there below, among the mortals,
> you are hope, its living spring.
> You, lady are so great, and so availing
> that whoever wishes grace without turning
> to you for it hopes to fly without a wing.
> Your benevolence not only helps the one
> who asks, but often it will run
> freely to be ahead of the petition.
> In you is mercy, in you is pity,
> in you is bounty, in you, brought together,
> all the good there is in any creature.

But, the St. Christopher medal held no religious connotations for me. It was a special gift from my brother, who in his own way was saying to me, "Please be safe." John still didn't freely express his sentiments. I was still puzzled by the fact that he didn't cry when Mommy, Daddy and Nonni Next Door died. He seemed to bottle everything up inside and I wanted to shout at him, "What kind of Italian are you? Why don't you yell and scream like the rest of us? Don't you know you'll blow some day if you don't?!" But, I said nothing. I hugged him tight, kissed him goodbye on the cheek and placed the medal in my glove box.

I felt sadness about leaving my friends, Nancy, Cheryl, Marshi and Karen. I would really miss them even when we just loafed around. It's sort of ironic that I never got to say goodbye to my friends in Torrington when I left— my godmother, Anne Favali and her son, Robbie, my best friend growing up. And all my other friends from childhood, Chris Mastro, Joni Marciano, Jimmy O'Brien, and my cousin Louie—and that was very painful. Now, I have the opportunity to say goodbye, but it feels just as painful. Yet, my friends in Newington were moving on in their own way, too. Nancy married Steve; I was her maid of honor (I told Nancy I hated that concept; it was so medieval and arcane, but because I was her best friend, I didn't really care what she called me). Marshi went off to college. Karen would be soon marrying Paul, a young civil war buff who her parents greatly approved of. In fact, I rarely saw Karen the summer after graduation, because she was always with Paul. I felt some resentment about this, feeling slightly abandoned by her, but I never spoke to her about it. I thought, "Well, if she doesn't have a need for our friendship anymore, than screw her." I wish I could have been more adult about it, because I would never see her again.

Cheryl wasn't engaged or getting married, but she started dating the Dustin Hoffman guy again. I said to her, "He's a jerk, Cheryl. Dump him before he really hurts you." She made me laugh when she responded sarcastically, "What, I should go back with some of the delinquents you tried to fix me up with?" Then Cheryl asked me, "Aren't you afraid about leaving on your own?" I said, "What could I possibly be afraid of? The worst is behind me. I don't think anything can ever hurt me anymore, at least not as badly." All my friends knew how rotten Mary and Bruno were, so they didn't question my desire to get away. I still couldn't bring myself, however, to tell any of them the full ugly story.

And, I didn't tell them my biggest fear; that, despite my cache of old photographs I might forget what my parents looked like as I moved forward in life. There seemed to be such a distance between my life in Torrington, which ended at thirteen, or perhaps eleven years old, and my life now. It felt like a completely different lifetime. But, I never want to lose or forget the life I had with my parents and grandmothers. I think it might be the happiest time I will ever know. I try to keep my paternal grandfather and Uncles Freddy and Livio and Aunts Pauline and especially Gloria into that picture but somehow they get squeezed out, because I can no longer remember the contentment and comfort they once brought, but only the pain they caused my Dad, and in turn, my brothers and me.

I don't doubt the love they once had for my parents, brothers, and me but rather questioned how devotion, loyalty and caring can so quickly evanesce from a family landscape. A series of endless questions barraged me:

"Can't they remember that we are the offspring of their once much-loved Tosca and George?"

"What have we done that was so terribly wrong?"

"Didn't they realize that their transgressions against my two brothers and I defiled the memory of my parents?"

I realized that my aunts and uncles had, in effect, effaced the presence of my parents on this earth. I wondered how people like this measured their life's worth. Was it by the material wealth they had accumulated? Or is it by our capacity to give and be loved. At the risk of sounding schmaltzy, I have come to know that in our wanderings, it's not the possessions that make a difference. It's the people we meet along the way and how we are remembered by them. It is this that my parents gave to my brothers, their friends, and me. And, then, if only through their children and the other people whose lives they touched, will the memory of my parents be immortalized.

I knew that I would never see them again. In fact, my grandfather died in 1972, and no one bothered to tell my brothers and me until after he was buried. This was not in the least bit surprising, since the Riccucci's had obliterated us from their past and perhaps their future as well. Years later I learned from Lucia Rotondo that just before my father died, he confided a revelation to her—Dad finally came to know who was the true cause of the chasm in our family. It was his own father. Nonno was the instigator, the reason my grandmother had to leave and why the family exploded at the seams. I thought, almost disaffectedly, "It seems rather metaphorical that my Dad choose to shoot himself in his father's bedroom."

It was January 2nd and I was finally leaving. My TR-6 was packed with all my belongings and I had the remainder of my savings—about $2,000 dollars—in traveler's checks in my pocket. It was winter, but a balmy, sunny day of about 50 degrees with only a light, wispy dusting of snow on the ground. I had said my goodbyes to Ricci and my cousin John the night before. I was touched when John became nostalgic; but Ricci didn't seem to care at all. In the morning I said goodbye (read, good riddance) to Mary and Bruno and jumped in my car just as fast as I could. With my convertible top down, I peeled out and sped off.

But I was not alone. I could feel my Mom with me, protecting me. I knew since that day my Mom sat with me and translated the lyrics of my opera, *Norma*, that we would be connected for life. She had been with me all along. The bond between mother and daughter is so strong that even in death, it survives. And I feel great comfort in this, just as Norma did before she took her own life. She sings with Adalgisa in "*Mira o Norma*,"

Compagna tua m'avrai.
Per ricovrarci insieme
Ampia è la terra assai.
Teco del Fato all'onte
Ferma opporrò la fronte,
Finché il mio core a battere
Io senta sul tuo cor.

I have found my friend again.
For the rest of my life
I shall always stay with you.
The earth is big enough
To shelter us both from love.
Together with you, courageously,
We shall fight outrageous Destiny,
As long as in our breasts
Our loving hearts shall beat.